SMART PERMACULTURE DESIGN

Jenny Allen

Foreword by Bill Mollison

NEW HOLLAND

This book is dedicated to my Mum and Dad

Acknowledgements

Originally I put aside six weeks to take a few snippets from the garden and entwine them together in a little booklet. I have been so absorbed in the task that it's only recently I noticed two years have passed and those cuttings have taken root, spilling their digital blossoms into this beautiful book. Many people have poked seedlings into bare patches or helped me tie back scrambling vines and prune risqué branches.

Dean Cameron brings to the book his constant sense of wonder—finding fascinating things in the garden to ponder, discuss and photograph. He's patient enough to sit at the bedside of a caterpillar as it tragically gives birth to wasp larvae and catch stages of it on film.

Many other names should pop up in glowing letters as you catch a particularly interesting or witty phrase. Steven Lang's would pop up in lots of blank spaces as he took on the challenging role of corn-control—weeding out corny jokes. There may be a few he missed and I apologise if they have grown. Steven has also been a sturdy mentor and editor. My brother Richard and sister Juliet supported me in so many ways throughout the whole book. Judith Lukin-Amundsen helped to change the direction of the book in the early stages—from a political garden 'thriller' to one that focuses on pleasure and fun. A good move I trust. Bill Mollison was generous with his foreword; it reflects the book's spirit of wonder and contemplation.

Thanks to the crew at New Holland for their advice, support and design layout—Louise Egerton, Nanette Backhouse and Sam Chapman. Many other people have helped improve the text or provided technical information, including: Sammy Ringer, Mark Austin, Jane Cotter, Simone Dwyer, Annie Wall, Steve Wall, Morag Gamble, Barb Knudsen, Richard Piper, Ian Dooley, Frances Lang and Clayton Stokoe.

Steve Demasson drew all the wonderful sketches and cartoons. Michael Leunig was pleased his cartoon could take another wander through the fresh smell of new pages. Brian Rogers also helped capture some of the essence of the garden with photos.

The book follows the development of our garden and I'd like to thank many people who fertilised it with their ideas and irrigated it with their sweat, including: Dean, Rodney Castle, Steve Wall, Annie Wall, Barb Knudsen, Roger Westacott, Darin Earwicker and Annie Philp. If I missed anyone please come round to our place and the garden will show its appreciation with fruit.

Thank you all.

First published in Australia in 2002 by
New Holland Publishers (Australia) Pty Ltd
Sydney • Auckland • London • Cape Town
1/66 Gibbes Street Chatswood 2067 Australia
218 Lake Road Northcote Auckland New Zealand
86 Edgware Road London W2 2EA United Kingdom
80 McKenzie Street Cape Town 8001 South Africa

National Library of Australia Cataloguing-in-Publication Data:

Allen, Jenny.
    Smart Permaculture Design.

    Includes index.
    ISBN 9781877069178.

    1. Permaculture. I. Title.

    631.58

Publisher: Louise Egerton
Project Editor: Sam Chapman
Cover design: Jo Buckley and Karl Roper
Designer: Nanette Backhouse
Illustrator: Steve Demasson
Production Controller: Wendy Hunt
Reproduction: Colourscan, Singapore
Printer: Everbest Printing Co. Ltd (China)

10 9 8 7 6 5 4

Permaculture sees human civilisation for what it is — a mere strand in the web of life. By recognising this, we can coexist more harmoniously with nature, fostering a more stable global ecosystem. Philosophers Bill Mollison and David Holmgren articulated permaculture in the 1970s. They succinctly encapsulated the concepts of a permanent diverse and flourishing human culture and food web. Permaculture is built on design principles that are inspired by observing ecological systems and emulating them. These principles and a wide range of practical applications are relevant to all types of horticultural pursuits, from balcony gardening to the quarter-acre block and from small farms to large commercial enterprises. Permaculture is an ingenious way of life whose time has come. It is now practised in 120 countries.

The Summer Palace

Make a little garden in your pocket.
Plant your cuffs with radishes and rocket.
Let a passion fruit crawl up your thigh.
Grow some oregano in your fly.

Make a steamy compost of your fears.
Trickle irrigate your life with tears.
Let your troubled mind become a trellis.
Turn your heart into a summer palace

Michael Leunig

Foreword

Jenny (and Dean), as with all permaculture gardeners, having worked hard for two to three years, are relaxing into paradise.

In 'divine high-piping Pahlevi'[1] in the language of Persia (Iran), a garden is paradise; we would all agree!

At some stage, usually about years four to six, the gardener begins to realise that the garden they put in place with care, is doing something else, unplanned. Birds, the messengers of the forest, move in. Butterflies, delicate grace notes, enter the symphony that is a garden. Species of all continents make an accommodation with each other, and some species arrive unplanned.

Our gardens at Tyalgum in New South Wales, over five years, accumulated 106 species of birds, 20 or so reptiles, countless insects, and — soaring over the fish ponds — a pair of sea eagles. Drama, amusement, romance and beauty self-assembled before our eyes. From year four onwards, I would sit in the garden (no longer 'my' garden) and study it with a sense of wonder, never knowing what it would do next, or eventually.

Yet, despite this uncertainty, gardens planted in the permaculture mode yield and persist (even in our absence) for months and years, and do indeed provide excess food with minimal maintenance, and thus sustain and encourage contemplation.

The best thing about this account of paradise is that it is obviously built on a real experience, and has useful lists of plants, planning units and observations, all of which assist design.

I enjoyed the book and the illustrations.

Bill Mollison

Bill Mollison

[1] So described by Omar Khayam in his 'Rubaiyat'

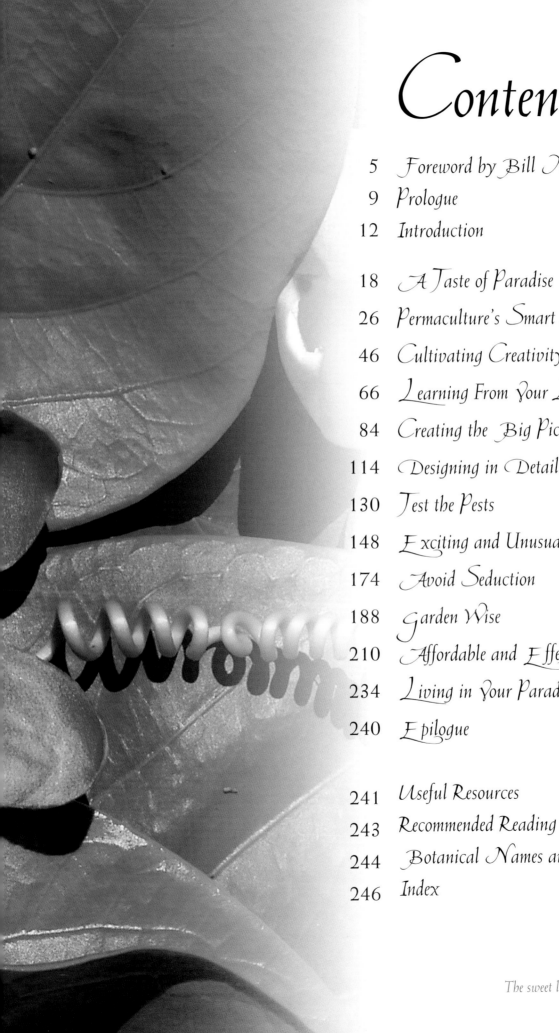

Contents

The sweet lillicoy passionfruit flower.

Prologue

Visions tend to intertwine. No sooner had I started sculpting a paradise in my garden than Dean, an inventor with a similar dream, began to help me shape it. Five years on, this happy meeting of a creative man of science and an innovative gardener has given rise to something larger than both of us. Radiating out from our house there is now a garden that provides us with almost everything we need: abundant and varied food, entertainment, tranquillity, living art and fascinating insights into nature.

The small green-banded blue butterfly.

Opposite: Our garden home.

After a hard day's work it's enchanting to throw myself into its green embrace. I climb wearily out of the car and my shoes crush the pennyroyal in the driveway, releasing the herb's minty aromatherapy, reminding me how great it is to be home. I step onto the verandah and I am enveloped by passion — or at least passionfruit — as the vine scatters its ripe fruit daily onto the hardwood boards. The red cherry guava tree cascades over the railings, enticing me with its burgundy red fruit.

There is a cacophony of shrieks coming from the Grevillea 'Honey Gem' — the rainbow lorikeets seem embroiled in more relationship dramas than a soap opera. I sometimes wish they, like TVs, also had a mute button.

To recharge, I pop a cherry tomato wrapped in basil into my mouth: it erupts with a flourish of zingy flavours.

Such abundance, and I've only got from the driveway to the verandah. I pluck some lemon verbena leaves and infuse them for a cup of tea. Beverage in hand, I wander out to the swinging chair.

I gently rock beneath the arching mulberry tree overlooking the dam. A gust of wind tosses the tops of the trees on the hill above. Here, in our lush green valley, all is tranquil. On the reflective surface of the dam, the green-tipped

One of our favourite characters in the impromptu garden comedy — the eastern water dragon.

branches of surrounding trees climb to an azure sky, then seemingly break into a million pieces with the passage of a wind-blown eddy from the hills above. Protected from the worst excesses of harsh weather, our garden is a snug nook.

The animals feel similarly protected. A water dragon lives among the rocks. Sometimes it is bold and will venture to my feet. Today it is pensive, watchful from beneath a grassy overhang. It's aware of my presence, flinching with every movement I make. I stop the motion of the chair. The water dragon seizes the moment. Shimmying up a craggy, sun-drenched rock, using its long tail to balance, it raises its head and puffs up the crest of spines on its neck, confident as a lion overlooking its domain...just for a moment. As I gently raise my cup of tea, it leaps into the water and disappears.

Dare to dream of your garden as a paradise.

Here in the green hills of Maleny, in sub-tropical Queensland, our little world is thriving. The region has waterfalls and rainforest creeks; just 30 kilometres away are the beautiful sandy beaches of the Sunshine Coast, and to the south-west, the eons-old Glasshouse Mountains stand sentinel in the afternoon sun. Queensland is often called 'paradise' and when I think about all that nature has to offer outside our front door, I smile in agreement. But I like to think that we have also helped create our own patch of heaven. While we are fortunate in where we live, the truth is that wherever you are, no matter where or what your plot of land may be, the most ordinary garden conceals a paradise within.

Introduction

One day I caught up with a friend who had taken to growing apples commercially. We walked through his orchard together, the rows of trees silent and graceful in the autumn light. I picked an apple and bit into its flesh, feeling like some latter-day Eve. Revelling in the taste, I turned to my friend and noticed that he was peeling his. I asked him why — didn't he like the skin? 'No,' he said, 'I never eat the skin; I know what's been sprayed on it.' My apple turned sour.

An artistic palette of magnolia pastels.

When it comes to killing pests, dragonflies have already clocked up millions of years' work experience and, with up to 30,000 eyelets each, they have adaptation on their side. Most importantly, they're hungry.

I had always wanted to live in a home that was a fertile oasis, a place to communicate with nature, one that would provide me with lots of fresh healthy food and meet my creative needs. That day in the orchard I realised that the development of such a paradise was a more intricate process than I had first imagined.

Looking around I noticed many gardens were not well thought out, often suffering from dry soil, overbearing weeds or lots of pests. Many were dependent on humans scrambling around spraying and cutting — such intensive labour didn't ensure fruitful results. Humans rarely match the work of nature where such beneficial predators as dragonflies, for instance, dart around to catch pests on the wing.

I knew instinctively that there had to be a better way; that with a broader understanding of nature we should be able to develop a productive garden that was also free from poisons. Once I started looking, I found there *were* other ways.

Some of the knowledge has been available for centuries; some of it has only recently been discovered — how, for example, insects and plants and soil relate to each other — but only a few people were looking at the whole system and how it interconnects in something as simple as a garden. I wanted to include all of those things, as well as joy and pleasure.

Permaculture encapsulated everything I was seeking. A permaculture garden is a designed ecology based on natural principles. It looks at a garden as a whole, not just at its parts. It's not just a collection of plants, but an integrated community within which humans have a sense of place.

It's smart. A permaculture garden is designed to be cleverer and more self-reliant than the average garden. It has the diversity, strength and flexibility of a natural ecosystem and can therefore rely on its native instinct. It harmoniously weaves together animals, plants, wind, frost, soil, structures, sun—and harnesses their potential uses so that they do the bulk of the work for you, the natural way. So what humans enjoy least — the gardening slog — is often reduced or done for free.

Good design minimises weeds, pests and the need to water, while improving the soil and sensory delight. Permaculture calls on nature's free gifts to reduce risk. Everything is placed in relation to everything else. The garden is zoned to reduce work and produce more. Plants and structures are recognised to have many uses, not just one. More is recycled and less brought in from outside. Diversity is highlighted and problems are turned into innovative, and sometimes wild, solutions.

At its most basic, permaculture provides a set of principles which can be applied to a garden to emulate the way nature works. This makes the garden more self-sufficient.

Paradise in Your Garden puts permaculture in simple terms that are relevant to all gardeners, whether starting from scratch or upgrading an existing garden. Its basic principles are applicable to any garden, be it large or small, in the tropics or in cool climates. Even gardens that seem unpromising present wonderful potential when viewed from a permacultural perspective.

A diverse and balanced garden creates niches for dazzling visitors, such as this sharp-eyed sacred kingfisher, which eats our grasshoppers.

The early part of this book presents permaculture's main design principles and the four important steps in planning a permaculture garden. The first involves visualising your dream and letting your imagination fly. The second is understanding your land. The third and the fourth delve into the finer details of design to help bring your dream to fruition. This part also alerts you to potential problems, a component many gardening books tend to play down.

The latter part of the book focuses on smart gardening. It includes techniques to save time and effort while not setting off the wallet alarm.

Most of the plants I recommend are appropriate for a wide range of areas. Of course, there are exceptions…the miracle fruit tree is such a surprising plant I couldn't resist including it. However, it's quite specific in its needs: a warm, humid area protected from hot sun, frost and wind. The section on creating beneficial

micro-climates explains how to develop a variety of conditions in your garden to broaden the range of species you can grow. You may just be able to experience the miracle.

I've avoided recommending many species that are potential weeds or, in some cases, have given warnings. The subject of rampancy is a difficult one. I wanted to recommend plants that grow well—just not so well that they take over. On page 244–45 I've indicated plants that are potential weeds in some areas with an asterisk. As rampancy is often site-specific, it helps to be aware of your local conditions, and plant and manage accordingly. When in doubt, go native.

Every photo in this book was taken within 50 metres of our house (except the mushroom letterbox). Many of them are designed to show how small, but significant, changes can be achieved with imagination and a constant focus on two permaculture themes: usefulness and pleasure.

I wrote *Paradise In Your Garden* to inspire readers who want to make their garden organic, fruitful and exciting, and also to impart some of the wisdom

Oblivious to the permaculture paparazzi, the verdant katydid wanders out in her purple slippers.

we have accrued in hindsight. Hopefully it will guide you over the pitfalls we fell into. Our horticultural journey is one of almost comical trial and error. I have tried to be frank in disclosing its amusing (in retrospect) progress, weeds and all.

I hope my story inspires you to form a deeper connection with your land and that this book will bring home the essence of the relationship

Acerola cherries taste like strawberries yet are more prolific. They have fewer pests and, being perennial shrubs, they're less work.

between your land and your garden. I hope above all that it will stimulate you into making your garden more luxurious, providing an oasis when the world turns into a dry argument.

A Taste of Paradise

At times creating a paradise may feel like a hard slog.
Yet for me it only takes the taste of a hand-picked pineapple
guava, the colourful splash of a new bird species moving in,
or the feel of winter sun radiant on my back as I drink tea in
the garden, and I'm assured that it is this world of peace,
harmony and intrigue I want to live in. Come with me this
particular Sunday morning for a stroll through the garden
to gather exotic food for a banquet lunch.

*Crazed floral sparks radiate
hints of the coming passion.*

*I*t is a clear and brisk May morning; filtered light stretches through in golden shafts. The orange tree swells its sunshine orbs with sweet nectar. Immediately next to it the mulberry tree has begun to hibernate. Its leaves are shrivelling, brown and brittle. Its life is now a rehearsal for death. These two trees are responding to the one season...nature balancing opposites. In a similar way we strive to balance the ideal and the practical; the ends and the means; paradise and the carting of mulch to create it.

Today I will follow the path of the orange tree. It is to be a day of plenty. There is an old Sanskrit saying: 'Atithi Devo Bhava', 'A guest is equal to God'.

Five guests are coming, all with supernatural appetites.

The recipes for today's banquet will be determined by what's in season. I tentatively consider the possibilities of a dip, an Australian frittata, a Greek salad with exotic accessories, a chocolate pudding fruit mousse, fruit salad and an Australian summer pudding.

Once I'm in the vegetable garden I'm likely to be sidetracked. So I head resolutely to where I'll harvest the appetiser. From there I shall pluck my way through to dessert. Let's see what's in the Green Pages when I let my taste buds do the walking.

The grandest book of all, I mean the Universe, stands open before our eyes. Leonardo da Vinci

Juicy blood oranges have a hint of aniseed and extend the citrus season.

A flower garden with vegies or a vegie garden with flowers?

Sunlight coalesces into deltas of Ruby Red chard.

Eggplants abound — so I'll roast these with the enormous Russian garlic which I've stored from last season, and blend them to make the dip. Fortunately this garlic has a subtle flavour or we'd be stripping the paint off the wall with mere light conversation.

This dense and delectable dip should be scooped with something light. Fresh slivers of the crisp Yucon tuber will be perfect. Until recently, this was a rarity in Australia but now it is becoming more accepted. It is easily cultivated, produces lots of crunchy tubers and tastes like a delicious mix of apple and carrot.

Let's wander into the main course zone. The frittata will use a lot of garden produce: potatoes, spring onions, society garlic, marjoram, Ruby Red chard and Australia's native spinach— Warrigal greens. Early settlers in Australia were so busy attempting to recreate Britain that local food and flavours were usually overlooked. This situation has barely improved. While Warrigal greens are a regular on many tables of Mediterranean Europe, wheat farmers out west spray them as a weed.

Two red capsicums, combined with a hint of the perennial chilli capsicum, will boost the colour and flavour of the frittata — chargrilled, pureéd and then drizzled over the top.

The Greek salad will include a variety of atypical greens: the leafy mushroom plant tastes like mushrooms; the sweet leaf bush tastes like young peas; and the Lebanese cress tastes like carrot. These will be combined with lettuce and other goodies, and placed on top of fiery rocket to lift the flavour to the stars.

My taste buds, best friends of the inner child, are aroused by the prospect of dessert. Last week, I harvested five chocolate pudding fruits: they need about seven days to ripen. They're ready

Society garlic: the whirling lilac fairies grant your wish for garlic flavouring without the accompanying bad breath.

when they turn marshmallow soft and mocha brown. Blended with yoghurt, honey and vanilla they make a healthy and, most importantly, a tasty, full-bodied chocolate mousse.

The dependable babaco will be the heart of the fruit salad. It originally came from the highlands of Ecuador. While not as sweet as

Fuschia and chilli capsicum jostle together harmoniously.

pawpaw, it's a sadly neglected cousin. Give it the attention it deserves and its tangy flavour will romance the palate taking your memory for a walk down pineapple and strawberry lane.

To ginger up the occasion I add robust flavours. Following a piquant trail I allow my steps to be guided by my nose towards the creamy white guavas. The aroma from just one of these fruits can decorate a room. Shops and supermarkets rarely supply these guavas (in fact they rarely stock any of the items I'm harvesting today) as they have little hard seeds and their shelf life would probably have to be improved by implanting a gene from a radiantly aging old woman (someone for whom being left on the shelf was a career move).

My Australian summer pudding will be an adaptation of the traditional English one. It will use fruits with vivid colours, notably the vibrant red native raspberries. I bought the raspberry canes five years ago from an Aboriginal group in northern New South Wales. They selected and

cultivated native varieties of plants to produce bigger and tastier fruit. They have succeeded with panache.

I go to the kitchen to mix and match the day's harvest. A number of ingredients which we've cultivated and stored need to be brought into play. Included are items we've bought. I'm not sufficiently focused to make it all from the garden. It's possible, of course, but trying to be fully self-sufficient can turn gardening from a delight to a chore.

I cover the table with sizable banana leaves and make a display for the centre out of a water-filled dish complete with colour-splashed flowers and floating candles.

The guests arrive hungry.

The yucon tuber is splayed around the roasted eggplant-and-garlic dip. The Warrigal greens, olive-and-fetta frittata is drizzled with roasted red capsicum sauce and given a finishing sprinkle of native pepper. The Greek salad is a festival of greens, fetta, artichokes and roasted walnuts.

As the laugh-o-meter reaches maximum decibels, the fruit salad is mixed with nuts and dressed with a dash of Cointreau. The chocolate pudding fruit mousse is covered with shaved chocolate and the colourful Australian summer pudding is served with creamy macadamia nut ice-cream.

🐚

These garden delights raise the curiosity of our guests, which is fun, but not the only reason to grow them. The main reason is that they are easy to produce, resistant to pests and diseases, often

Iridescent native raspberry plants selected and enhanced by an Aboriginal bushfood co-op.

To make a healthy chocolate pudding fruit mousse, mix equal parts flesh and yoghurt, honey to taste and a dash of vanilla or rum. Decorate with strawberry colours and chocolate surprises.

food is often designed primarily to travel and keep: tomatoes that can be harvested by machine, dropped onto a conveyor belt and then sent across the country. They no longer even splat when you drop them — in fact, they could have rubber-tree genes spliced into them as they seem to just bounce.

Often supermarkets are designed with seduction areas at the furthest points of their perimeter so customers trek all the way around. The perimeter is where their high profit items are. They also entice people to lap the aisles so that they are exposed to as many products as possible.

A permaculture garden is laid out differently. It's designed for the least work and the maximum gain. Today's banquet was all harvested from within 25 metres of the front door — and is as fresh as can be.

Just wait until you taste it.

difficult to buy fresh in the shops and, most importantly, they're tasty. Diversity is the spice of life and one of the main principles of permaculture.

Sadly, the world seems to be heading the other way. Many supermarkets focus little on variety, flavour, aroma or nutrition as their 'fresh'

In autumn I start 'bandicooting' around the yukon plants for large tubers and orange-tinged flesh. Tubers harvested earlier in the year are smaller and not as sweet.

Permaculture's Smart Design Principles

Permaculture is an ingenious design system based on working in harmony with nature. It looks at a garden as a whole, not just at its parts. Everything interrelates. In return, the garden treats you as a whole (and a hedonist). It pleases not only your tastebuds, but rewards your eyes, ears, nose and soul as well.

We step off our verandah into the salad bowl.

A permaculture garden helps cater for many of its own needs, such as soil management, weed control, mulch production, water conservation and pest management. For instance, instead of killing aphids with poisonous sprays, the permaculture garden is designed to entice ladybirds to eat them.

I am strongly of the opinion that a quantity of plants however good the plants may be themselves and however ample their number, does not make a garden; it only makes a collection. Gertrude Jekyll

They do it skilfully — it's their living art — turning dishwater green aphids into their own vivid red-with-black polka dots.

At its most basic, permaculture is based on 10 fundamental principles.

I use these principles constantly. They keep me on track; they're my gardening angels, preventing me from making painful oversights, piloting me towards effective design. In conjunction with understanding the land, the principles help me save time and money.

Whenever I am designing a garden I go through the principles step-by-step and a blueprint miraculously emerges for me to work with. I use them again at the end of the process as a checklist. They ensure things are placed effectively and help avoid disasters.

Some people baulk at the idea of imposing rules, especially when it involves a fun part of life such as gardening — perhaps it reminds them too much of school or work. But you probably already use some of the principles without realising it. If you have

Birds are good pest-control agents. This tawny frogmouth eats a lot of insects such as crickets and beetles.

The blue triangle butterfly.

How Permaculture Emulates Nature

Nature	A Routine Garden	A Permaculture Garden
Self-maintaining	Maintenance burden	Designed for little maintenance
Pests balanced	Often pests and poisons	Integrated Pest Management (see page 146)
No irrigation	Guzzles water	Strategies save water
Lots of uses	Few functions	Pampers many needs
Many layers	Few layers	Layer upon layer upon layer
Few extremes	Exposed to weather	Cooler summers/warmer winters
Diverse	Few species	Lots of exciting plants and animals
Costs zilch	Like a moth in the wallet	Uses less money

herbs in a window box or pot outside the kitchen, then you're using the Zoning Principle. If you have tomatoes and basil side-by-side, you're using both the Multiple Uses and Using Nature's Gifts principles: tomatoes and basil go naturally together in salads and sauces, and the basil helps keep your tomatoes free from grubs. Do you have a windbreak deflecting harsh westerlies? Three uses for the big mulberry tree? Or a dam in place of a sludgy swamp? If so, you've already instinctively incorporated some of the 10 Design Principles into your garden. And you're probably using more than you initially realise. Some of the design principles, you may notice, overlap.

Permaculture favours perennial plants because annuals are a lot of work. They open the garden up to weeds, they need a lot of water and their continual replacement means you and nature have to keep starting over and over again. Perennials have deeper root systems enabling them to access nutrients and water more efficiently. They also create long-term beneficial micro-climates, are more pest resistant and can be used in many ways throughout their lifecycle. It's tempting to go for the fast splash of colour and quick food that annuals provide, so for short-term pleasure and long-term ease permaculture principles recommend a combination of short-term plants that you really want mixed with many long-term productive plants.

Each permaculture principle can be applied to the garden as a whole, or to a part of it. Some people apply these principles to more than just their gardens. They can be useful in almost any field...cooking and kitchen management, business, bringing up children. Nature's blueprint is adaptable if we stretch our imagination.

Banana plants provide a quick staple food and bear flowers that attract honeyeaters.

Our Garden: Before and After

One of the major problems I inherited when I bought this property was the weed-infested swamp, which bred mosquitoes (see below). We replaced the swamp with a multi-functional dam that incorporates all permaculture's design principles (see bottom photo). Water stores the sun's energy and gradually lets it out, stabilising the temperature of the land around it. The oranges on the dam wall receive good drainage; the cocoyams at the water's edge are passively

irrigated; the palms and reeds help clean the water; the fish convert other people's waste into food; the warmer micro-climate means we can grow more vulnerable tropical plants; and the swinging-chair nearby is a ringside seat to watch it all happen — while eating mulberries. Throughout the book you'll see other principles we incorporated around the dam.

The 10 Smart Design Principles

The 10 Smart Design Principles bring a different, and altogether broader, perspective to gardening. I've included examples to help explain each of them; gardens, however, vary tremendously, so some of these examples may not suit your specific conditions. What is important is the principle, not the example.

The arrowroot border at the top of our vegie garden.

1. Multiple Uses

A basic premise of permaculture is that most things in the garden should serve at least three purposes. This makes the garden significantly more useful and abundant. (Although I believe beauty in itself is enough reason for some plantings.)

For instance, if you plant an arrowroot edge along the top of your vegetable garden, it can serve up to eight purposes. It keeps out invading grass and weeds, provides a decorative border, adds lushness and its tubers are edible. It also serves as a habitat for beneficial predators, such as frogs, and as a screen to give privacy and reduce the impact of wind. When the risk of damaging winds has passed, it can be cut back for valuable mulch; then it will regrow. If necessary, pull out tubers entering the garden once a year.

The trees on our western boundary have many uses. We selected particularly bushy ones to: help reduce the impact of the westerlies; stop passerbys looking in, block some of the traffic noise and they're fire retardant to help reduce the chances of fire.

Oranges also have many uses. After eating them we dry their skins on the fire and they

If designed well, wetlands and boggy areas can have many uses. Plants, such as these native palms and swamp lilies, filter excess nutrients that would otherwise pollute. They give refuge for wildlife, as well as being attractive.

infuse the house with a delicious orange aroma. The next day we use the dried skins as oil-rich firelighters.

2. The Zoning Principle

Dividing areas of the garden into zones, numbered according to their proximity to the house, cuts down effort while achieving maximum return. In Zone 1, which is closest to the house, place what you visit most such as the clothesline and herb garden. While smaller gardens may only have one or two zones, larger properties may go up to Zone 5. As you go further afield, the required maintenance of structures and plants diminishes and nature plays a larger role.

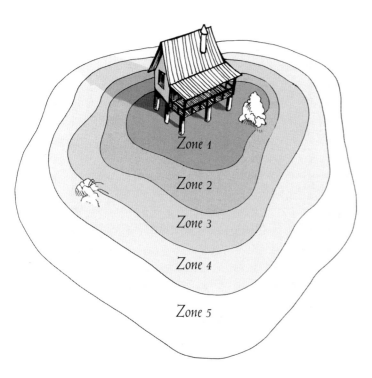

Zone 1

Zone 2

Zone 3

Zone 4

Zone 5

ZONE 1: This area closest to the house is the most visited and often requires the most maintenance. There may be trellises built onto the house, a barbecue, the clothesline and the compost. You might like to have a shaded seat and a kaffir lime for Thai curries. Being close to the house, you can nip out in your fluffy slippers to pick a few of its leaves for a late-night curry. An entire herb garden is useful here for the same reason, as well as vegetables that you pluck often, such as lettuces and cherry tomatoes. As we frequently pluck our organic herbs, they are grown close by on the verandah in our natural hydroponic system.

ZONE 2: Zone 2 is an area for vegetables and for fruits that are picked often, like lemons and strawberries.

A pecan tree.

An apple.

ZONE 3: This zone suits a shade tree, smaller bush foods and medium-sized fruit trees, such as oranges, nectarines and apples. Between the fruit trees grow edible groundcovers like pumpkins and pepinos.

ZONE 4: This zone has larger fruit trees, such as rose apples, persimmons and avocados; nut trees such as macadamias and pecans; larger bush foods; and firewood and cabinet timbers.

ZONE 5: Leave this to nature to regenerate — it's a quiet place to meditate and learn how the vegetable and animal kingdoms inter-relate. If weeds are a problem, you may need to help manage them initially.

3. Smart Placement

Place elements in the garden where many of their needs are met and they meet some of your needs as well. If a tree drops its leaves and rotten fruit, then place the tree in the chicken pen so it feeds the chickens rather than littering a prize lawn. It will then, in turn, be fed naturally by the chicken manure.

We grow prickly plants along the steep embankment to stop the children taking a dangerous short-cut to the dam.

Umbrella-shaped trees shade our driveway. Strawberries are planted on the lower edge of the sandstone pavings so they get radiant heat and are irrigated by extra water run-off.

A fragrant gardenia nearby masks the smell of the scrap bucket. Toss one in after cleaning it…

Some people bribe children with sweets — we tried it on the bees in a desperate attempt to entice them to pollinate the passionfruit. Like most bribery, it didn't work.

4. Elevational Planting

Calculate the effects of your land's elevation. If you have an incline in your garden, figure out what differences there are between the lowest and highest points. There may be differences in soil types and moisture levels, water run-off, wind exposure, humidity levels, sun angles, temperature and frost susceptibility.

Even if your garden is flat, you still need to take height into account: tall things can affect the availability of sunlight. For example, place smaller plants to the north, facing the winter sun. Further to the south, they can be correspondingly larger. That way all the plants will get reasonable amounts of sunlight. If you're in the northern hemisphere, do the opposite.

If your garden slopes, grow trees like olives, mulberries and loquats at the top of the slope, as these can handle the wind and drier soil. Grow sensitive plants further down so they will be protected from the wind and nurtured, not only by higher humidity, but also by more soil moisture and nutrients. If they don't like frost, divert it with a frost barrier (see page 112).

The top spot on the dam wall goes to the citrus as they enjoy good drainage. The bananas are planted lower as they love the extra moisture and sheltered micro-climate.

5. Recycling Resources

Rather than continually buying valuable resources from outside, try to retain as many as possible in the garden. Unplanned gardens can be net nutrient losers. Three common problems are loss of nitrogen into the air, the erosion of nutrient-rich soil and water run-off. Like money, it can be a lot more difficult to create resources than to simply save them in the first place.

So, rather than having your compost heap in an unused corner of the garden, place it instead at the top of your vegetable garden. Gravity and rain will leach its valuable nutrients down to the hungry vegetables. After you've brought in the harvest, feed the vegetable scraps to the chickens, and scatter their manure on the vegie patch to grow more vegetables. Harvest again, feed the scraps to the chooks again…thus the cycles of life keep turning.

The fleshy stems of bananas suck up water and nutrients. After fruiting they are cut and recycled as mulch.

6. Growing Up

Nature has a complex design already planned for your land. The more you understand her ecological blueprint and the more closely you emulate that plan, the less effort and disappointment. If left to her own devices, nature would, in many cases, gradually change from grass to so-called 'weed' species, from there to short-term 'pioneer' bushes, and finally to a mixture of mainly long-term large 'climax' trees. At this end stage nature is most bounteous.

Although this free-for-all is more productive, it does not always suit us. Most people love their lawn, despite lawn being nature at her most inefficient: it requires relentless work to keep a monoculture curtailed. Rather than wage an ongoing battle with nature, look to compromise by growing productive, long-term plants, for example fruit trees and cabinet timbers, in appropriate places, as well as keeping a handy patch of lawn.

If you're fond of your fruit trees, as we are, plan your plantings to achieve successive yields. To satisfy a fast-fruit frenzy grow a lot of speedy fruiters like babacos and tamarillos. As these are short-lived, averaging a few years, strategically plant longer-term fruit trees around them, like carambola and avocado. While the short-termers are bursting with food, they're also supplying mulch, humidity and protection for the long-termers. When they die, the long-termers take over. This uses the natural growth habits of plants — how fast they'll grow and fruit, how large they'll grow, how long they'll live and all their functions — to help nature perform effectively.

Permaculture encourages synergies between annual and perennial plants to more efficiently use the soil profile, sunlight, water and labour. It also plans ahead — this blue quandong is just one of the cabinet timbers that will be ready to harvest in 25 years.

Lawn is nature under totalitarian rule. Michael Pollan

7. Diversity

A wide variety of plants ensures interesting food all year round. With careful placement, different plants can work together to help protect each other from weeds, frost, heat and wind. And if a plant-specific pest attacks one plant, diversity means many more will still produce.

Ten years ago, normally dignified dinner guests would discretely sneak more than their fair share of avocado from the salad. Now that avocados are considered common, they're not so enticing and rarely provoke such embarrassing behaviour. It seems that food items increase in value and importance if they are considered rare. Spend less money by growing more unusual plants such as feijoas (pineapple guavas) — one of my favourites. Each fruit sells for about 70 cents in the shops.

Even within a single species there are many varieties. For example, five different types of oranges may fruit over six months — some will

Nature pioneered the art of creative and biodegradable packaging.

keep well, some won't, some are for juicing, others for eating fresh, others are ideal for making marmalade.

According to the Digger's Club Seed Catalogue, today we only disseminate 3% of the variety of seeds our grandparents propagated. Mass-marketing has resulted in us missing out on many delicious fruits. Mulberries and raspberries, for example, don't package, travel or store well so food companies tend to ignore them. More's the pity because these types of fruit are often the most succulent. Today, the greatest source of diversity in our streamlined processed food industry is not so much in the food as in its packaging.

Sweeter and larger than a grapefruit, pomelos add diversity to a garden and the palate.

8. Homemade Insurance

Reduce dependence on conventional insurance by devising your own Garden Insurance Policy. Analyse what elements are the most vital to you, such as water, food year round and fire protection. Then, if possible, create a range of ways to deliver each one of them.

For instance, don't rely on just one source of water, in case there's a hitch. Maybe you could incorporate swales, terraces, mulch to keep moisture in the soil, diversion drains, a water tank or two, or a large dam.

For a steady harvest of food, grow a range of hardy crops that fruit all year round and disperse them throughout the garden. If some crops fall prey to adverse conditions, such as high winds or hungry pests, the others are positioned where they are likely to survive.

If fire is a threat, have a lawn with a road around it on the most vulnerable side of the house to act as a fire barrier. Plant fire-resistant trees as the castle walls; these can double as a windbreak. In the fire-prone Dandenongs in Victoria, a smart man incorporated many of these safety strategies and more. When bushfires scorched their way through his area, his house and garden survived, even though his doormat was smouldering on his return. Sadly, many of his neighbours' homes were burnt.

The importance of reducing the chances of your house and land being burnt has become more obvious since the fires raged through Sydney and surrounding areas. Together with the

Lots of young eucalypts were growing around the house when I first came. I quickly replaced them with plants that don't mature into potential fireballs.

family think of a range of strategies you could incorporate to reduce potential fire damage.

It pays to be ingenious and enact your own insurance (with no small print).

9. Using Nature's Gifts

Nature offers such bounty, yet often it is little appreciated. If we understand her ways, we can learn to work with her wisely. She is willing not only to work for us, but to provide things that otherwise we would resort to bringing in from outside. After regenerating for millions of years, nature has the experience, and can prove it by often doing a better job than we can. So think re-creatively and devise some activities for her.

There are potentially millions of workers ready to help you with your gardening unpaid if you just provide for their needs. Worms—one of the strongest creatures for their bodyweight —and micro-organisms will help improve your soil. Predators of pests, such as lacewing larvae

If you provide the right conditions, hoverflies will move in and eat aphids, beetles and caterpillars.

Look for nitrogen-fixing plants that thrive in your area, such as this crotalaria does in ours.

and ravenous assassin bugs, will devour copious numbers of pests such as thrips. But watch out: if their needs are not met—shelter, food, water and safety—they are quick to stage a walkout. Or a wiggleout.

Give a fruit tree a boost by planting around it small nitrogen-fixing bushes, such as tagasaste, pigeon pea or crotalaria, as well as a nitrogen-fixing groundcovers, such as pinto peanuts or clover. Such plants help feed the tree, reduce the grass and weeds, and are a great source of mulch.

As your imagination stretches, so will nature's largesse—try using banana leaves as picnic placemats and then simply mulch the garden with them when the party's over. No washing up!

10. See Solutions, Not Problems

If you have a problem area in the garden, see how you can transform it into something positive. Using a creative frame of mind, your predicament will often present you with an opportunity to develop something new and special that you might never otherwise have thought of. Rather than looking on a boggy patch as a blot on the landscape, look to it as an ideal site for a dam. A shady area can be turned into a fernery. That ugly fence is crying out to support a passionfruit vine.

A shady area is an opportunity to create a more lush mood.

Waterlilies automatically come up in our dam and initially I saw this as a problem because they prevented any slime escaping over the spillway. But now we have cleaned out just those lilies in front of the spillway and the other lilies actually help to keep the slime down by using up excess nutrients and by providing habitat for fish that eat it.

You can even adapt this last permaculture principle to achieve a more cooperative life…

In the middle of difficulty lies opportunity. Albert Einstein

An edible Asian water garden was our solution to a boggy problem.

The Design Principles in Action

Before...

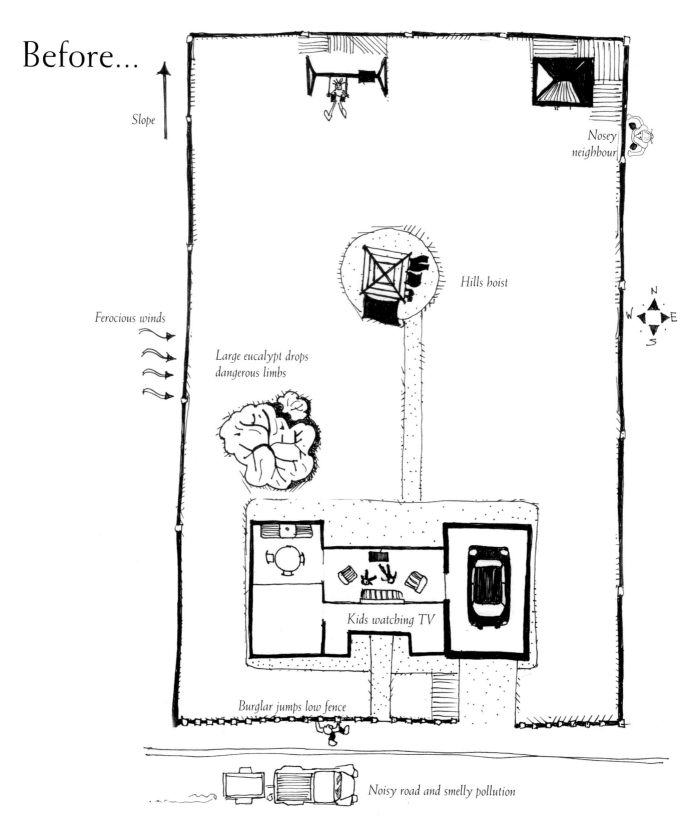

Slope

Ferocious winds

Nosey neighbour

Large eucalypt drops
dangerous limbs

Hills hoist

Kids watching TV

Burglar jumps low fence

Noisy road and smelly pollution

...and After

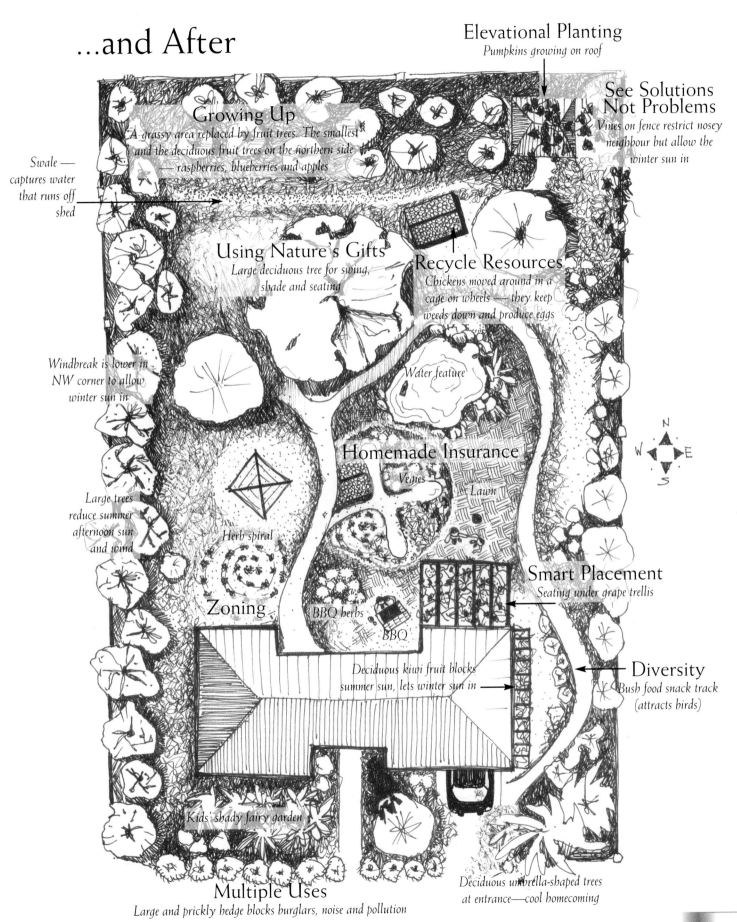

Elevational Planting
Pumpkins growing on roof

See Solutions Not Problems
Vines on fence restrict nosey neighbour but allow the winter sun in

Growing Up
A grassy area replaced by fruit trees. The smallest and the deciduous fruit trees on the northern side — raspberries, blueberries and apples

Swale — captures water that runs off shed

Using Nature's Gifts
Large deciduous tree for swing, shade and seating

Recycle Resources
Chickens moved around in a cage on wheels — they keep weeds down and produce eggs

Windbreak is lower in NW corner to allow winter sun in

Water feature

Homemade Insurance

Vegies

Lawn

Large trees reduce summer afternoon sun and wind

Herb spiral

Zoning

Smart Placement
Seating under grape trellis

BBQ herbs

BBQ

Deciduous kiwi fruit blocks summer sun, lets winter sun in

Diversity
Bush food snack track (attracts birds)

Kids' shady fairy garden

Multiple Uses
Large and prickly hedge blocks burglars, noise and pollution

Deciduous umbrella-shaped trees at entrance—cool homecoming

Cultivating Creativity

Spark your imagination. Dream a garden full of potential, not limitations; one that meets many of your needs, while pampering some desires as well. Select from 64 imaginative — and some wild — ideas of what it could contain. The ideas are grouped in themes that can make a real difference in life — entertainment, tranquillity, kids' enjoyment, fascinating foods, beauty, wildlife, cultural and medicinal gardens, creativity and aromatic surprise...the ingredients for pleasure, pleasure, pleasure.

Cactus boots.

There was once a famous landscape architect, 'Capability' Brown. His pseudonym arose from his ability to transform a landscape, no matter how barren or seemingly impossible. He would characteristically declare: 'This has capability!'

He could see the potential in any wasteland — and create a masterpiece. Where others saw limitations, Capability Brown saw potential. At this stage, dare to dream. Ignore those voices that say 'This will never work'. Allow yourself to play. Limitations can cloud your vision and are often the result of low expectations. It's surprising how little people want from their garden and how much from their 'plug-in drugs': videos, video games, computers, the telephone and television. Home entertainment systems offer a shallow experience compared to the creative stimulation of gardening.

By exploring your fertile imagination your garden can become a positive extension of yourself. Are you, for example, fun loving? Does this show in your garden? Are you a great cook — with lots of different herbs and vegies that you can pluck as you need? Do you love history — and grow fascinating plants that date back to the dinosaur era, such as the bolwarra? Do you like to surprise and test people — with flavours like that of the peanut butter fruit?

What are you really like — and does your garden reflect this?

Life shrinks or expands in proportion to one's courage.
Anais Nin

Even the water dragon is bewildered.

Plants growing up an attractive spiral trellis help protect heat-sensitive plants, such as coriander and lettuce, from the hot sun.

Unleashing the Imagination

Allowing your dreams to unfold is an important exercise. Without dreams what are the chances of their fulfilment? Making lists and drawing ideas and plans helps to solidify thoughts, bringing them a step closer to reality.

I have drawn the following inference, that the limits to pleasure are as yet neither known nor fixed. Brillat Savarin

To help develop your own garden wish-list, start with some Aspirational Trees. I recommend a large piece of paper and lots of colourful textas or pencils. Around the page draw bubbles. Leave room between the bubbles for branches to come out. Write in the bubbles the things that are important to you in life; examples might be: tranquillity, entertainment, good food and happy kids. Branching out from each of the bubbles, write down anything you could create in your garden that would help you to achieve these. At this stage don't worry if they're possible or where they would go in the garden. Be sure to list all possibilities, even those that seem unlikely. Some of these may later be quashed by practicalities but the more exciting possibilities you have to work with at this stage, the better. Then go through the wish-list on pages 52–65 and add some more ideas.

Another useful exercise to inspire creativity is a visualisation. Visualisation is an old technique used in many philosophies, religions and lifestyles to both expand and concentrate the mind. This guided visualisation helps you dream up your perfect garden. Have some coloured pens and paper handy.

The graceful arches of the corduroy tamarind – a pretty rainforest tree with edible fruit.

Five Aspirational Trees

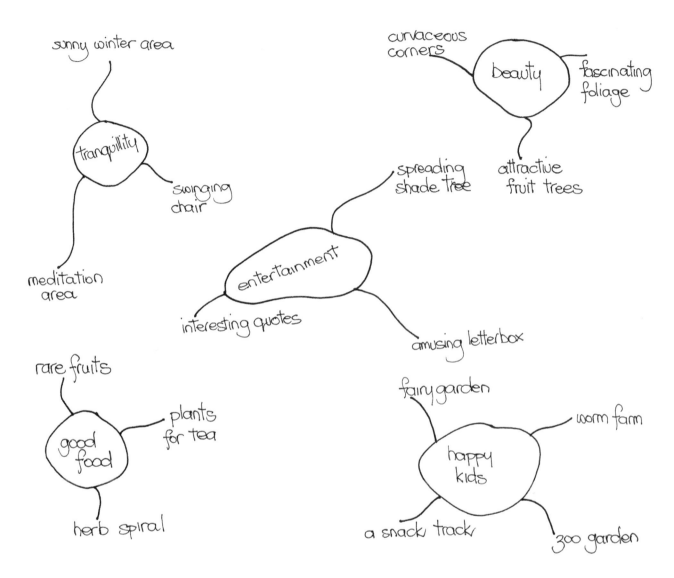

Put on some inspirational music. Sit down in a comfortable spot where you won't be interrupted. To help you 'see', shut your eyes. Imagine walking into your dream garden. (If possible, use your existing garden as a base.) Look around. Meander for as long as you want. Soak up the bliss. What's in it? How does it smell, taste and sound? How do you feel? What parts of it do you enjoy most? Keeping the special feelings with you, slowly come back to the present and where you are now.

Using your coloured pens, draw your dream garden. At this stage don't worry about where things should go — just let the feeling of lushness guide you.

As you draw, think about what ingredients you're adding to this garden pot-pourri. Choose ingredients that delight your passion and feed all your senses — sight, sound, smell, taste, feelings...

Ideas for Your Wish-list

Here are 64 features that could be included in your garden. Beside each one is a big leaf. Tick the leaves of those features which inspire you and add these to your own personal wish-list.

Tranquillise Yourself

Trees with an umbrella shape make for a pleasant entrance to your land. As you come home you can drive from hot sun into mottled shade — a welcoming arrival. Visitors can park comfortably in the shady drive.

Time to put your feet up? Care for a soothing swing?

A relaxing swinging-seat overlooking water or a wildlife area — with a bench on which to stand the regulation cup of tea.

A sunken garden is often circular, with mounds encircling it to deflect noise. It can resonate well with good acoustics if you play an instrument or sing. It's also a place to escape racket.

A hammock can be slung in dappled shade or sun, depending on the season — under a deciduous tree perhaps to make the most of all seasons. Surround it with edible plants such as apples, raspberries, strawberries, white

Our meditation seat.

micro-climate, i.e. little wind and radiated heat from a surface, such as rocks and walls. It's great if it gets sun all day but if not, try to plan both a morning and an afternoon sunspace. To allow winter sun in, plant deciduous fruit trees such as persimmon, apricot and Japanese raisin tree.

A FUNdamentalist's Garden

A fire circle brings the nocturnal tribe together. It's a great conversation stimulator: people gathering to watch the flames dance. This is often separate from the barbecue area, which is enclosed for heat retention and is generally more functional.

Collect quotes and have them inscribed and dotted around the garden. You might like to include stories about the garden…

A large shallow dish filled with water, interesting stones and candles. Float an array of delicate flowers or petals in it and display for a banquet.

An outside self-esteem bath, raised above ground to leave room for a fire underneath to warm the water. To avoid bottom-burning, lay wooden slats inside to sit on. Grow plants with aromatic flowers and leaves around so you can readily throw them in — lavender, jasmine, gardenia and mint. Lie back and stare at the stars as the steam rises around you. Don't fall asleep; unlike most baths these often get hotter not cooler. Start worrying when your friends throw in the vegies.

sapotes, cherry guavas and feijoas. Have a table nearby for your pina colada.

A quiet meditation area — surrounded by ambrosial scents such as lavender and rose geranium. This is best sheltered from bad weather, so that you can meditate daily without interruption. The time of day you like to meditate will determine where it is best situated. Surround it with objects that inspire reverence, such as statues, candles and incense. Let the family know this is where they can also disappear for quiet time.

A cool summer area in full shade that enjoys a water-splashed breeze and cool drinking water close by. Grow refreshing herbs to add to your drink, like lemon verbena, lemon balm and peppermint (in a pot to prevent rampancy). Design a shaded pathway to the house to avoid glaring sun while walking to and from.

Plan for some sunny seating areas for winter, with a warm

the scene. You could even integrate plants that suggest sexuality such as the philodendron, asparagus, the red hot poker or orchids whose flowers have feminine attributes. Some modern feminists might prefer the Venus fly trap.

The Kid's Tell-A-Vision

An amusing letterbox — ours is a red-capped *Amanita* mushroom (fly agaric) with little flecks of white on top. It's made from a rubbish bin, an old foam surfboard and bits of Styrofoam.

Surprise your postie – make a whacky letterbox.

Plant an aphrodisiac garden — a secluded nook hidden from noisy and nosey people. Out of the clash of sunlight and away from mosquitoes, nature's own acupuncturists. Leave room at the centre for two small heart-shaped gardens to join — maybe with a gracious statue of Venus blessing

Design the garden with the kids. What do they love to eat and what games do they like to play? Bring out the coloured textas and a big piece of paper and inspire them to draw what they want.

A kids' snack track to explore after school, and nibble straight off the plants: cherry tomatoes, snow peas, strawberries and asparagus.

Big climbing trees that bear enticing fruits or nuts, such as walnut and pecan.

Fruits that substitute for some of the sickly sweet nasties they may otherwise eat: Panama berries taste like chewing gum; mashed and frozen raspberries and strawberries can be eaten like iceblocks; and lemonade fruit can be eaten straight or made into a refreshing drink that beats cola.

Kids can give you playful ideas for the garden.

A kids' eating area in dappled shade, where it is okay for them to be messy, noisy and spill sticky things. Employ chickens to do the clean-up.

A worm farm. The worms eat the kitchen scraps; the kids have fun and you get the 'black gold'.

A giant outside draughts board or chessboard — make pieces to go on it, or play the game as a huge costume party. A ploy to educate kids in strategic thinking.

A sandpit with a hose nearby so children can wash off sand before coming into the house. When they grow out of it, convert it into a water feature.

A little amphitheatre for children to put on plays, or to have a sense of seclusion.

Fairy gardens filled with fairy flowers and coloured stones, shells and frog figurines, which they can dance around. Blueberry flowers look like delicate white ballerina skirts and citrus flowers look and smell pure.

A grassy patch for the kids to play. Plant hardy bushes around it which can survive the football and kids' trampling. Not the place for the exhibition roses.

Small animals for the kids to play with, such as pigeons, ducks, guinea pigs and chickens. The latter two can be kept in portable cages — 'chicken tractors' — which have mesh on the bottom and can be moved around to help mow the lawn.

A zoo garden with snake beans, dinosaur gourds, dragon fruit, coltsfoot, elephants' ears and tiger lily.

Little niches, with mazes, stepping stones and hidden paths to play hide-and-seek.

The scent of orange blossom is a time machine wafting me back to childhood.

Kids race around on a treasure hunt of wonder.

🌿 *A pet cemetery*. A tree can be planted and dedicated to each deceased pet. Also, the kids can include laminated (waterproofed) pet stories, poems, photos and drawings to help them remember where the pets are buried. You could place the cat under catmint, the lamb under lambs' ears and the dragon under snapdragons.

🌿 *Tree planting*. Each of the children plants a long-lasting tree and writes a poem about their future hopes to be time-capsuled under it or engraved and placed in front of it.

Beauty and the Feast

🌿 *Raise some heirloom plants from seed*, like the silky black Russian tomato and the Heirloom Italian Paste Mix of tomatoes. Many heirloom plants have been passed down by generations of families and friends, or by seed clubs. Start with easy crops such as lettuces and beans.

The jackfruit: bigger than a football, spikier than an echidna and some people think it tastes like a cross between the two. I love them.

Prove to sceptics that miracles do happen. Give them a miracle fruit to make sour food taste sweet.

🌿 *Try growing exotic fruits* unfamiliar to most. Two examples in our garden are the chocolate pudding fruit and the miracle fruit. The miracle fruit tree is not suited to all areas. It likes it warm and humid. In Australia, grow it in frost-free coastal regions as far south

The black Russian tomato.

as Sydney. It's such an amazing tree. For up to half an hour after eating the fruit everything you taste will be sweet, including olives and lemons.

Grow your own tea and coffee. Tea can be brewed from lemon verbena, lemon-scented myrtle, bergamot, mint and ginger.

Grow old regulars such as — dare I say it — chokos. But make a commitment to cook them in imaginative ways so, like my choko cheese pie, they become a treat not a form of torture (although this may be a matter of opinion).

Grow a variety of herbs and small vegies in pots, especially if you have limited cultivation space. Plant hardier species, such as parsley, coriander, rosemary and lettuce. Experiment with different shapes and forms. For example, lay a colourful cartwheel down, for a well-rounded design, and grow different herbs in each pie segment. A herb spiral creates dry and moist areas so you can plant herbs according to their needs (see pages 219).

All Things Bright and Beautiful

Obelisks, tall statues and tall skinny trees draw the eye upwards, especially in a small garden, creating a more expansive dimension.

Lanterns, candles and flares make a garden look more festive and are ideal for parties.

If you can't go out, go up. Add drama to a small garden with a cluster of tall skinny trees, such as this Mexican tree fern. Be aware some feature trees go through gawky stages — such as the Mexican tree fern in winter.

The Atherton almond is a stunning understorey plant
related to the macadamia and with edible nuts.

Choreographed velvet figurines of the native tamarind.

Grow plants with striking foliage, both for their imaginative shapes, such as the Atherton almond and native tamarind, and for colour.

Grow attractive fruit trees. Citrus have fragrant white flowers and wonderfully glossy leaves. The persimmon has orange fruit and deciduous foliage that also turns bright orange. Loquat and avocado trees have large tropical-looking leaves.

Making Scents

Line your pathways and drive with pleasant aromas at all heights. Be careful not to overdo it and end up with a mishmash. Rose geranium flowing onto the edges of the driveway exudes a sweet perfume whenever a car brushes past. On pathways, fill ugly gaps between pavers with pungent pennyroyal or thyme.

Dry your hankies on the lavender bush. This was the practice of the famous Australian landscaper, Edna Walling. Also, grow lavender to scent linen and insert sprigs in the pillow-slip to induce a peaceful sleep.

Plant rosemary and lavender near where you empty the compost bucket. Give the bucket a rough scrub with the rosemary sprigs, and then a light brush of lavender to remove the compost smells and leave it aromatic.

Rub your feet with pleasant-smelling herbs, like pennyroyal and thyme. Place them within easy reach of where you wash your feet or where you take off your shoes. Grow them under the washing-line so they release their fragrance as you walk over them. Pennyroyal can become rampant so grow it in confined spaces.

The evocative scent of the gardenia stirs sweet emotions.

Grow a fragrance garden, such as a Lemon Garden, with lemon balm, lemon basil, lemon verbena, lemon grass, lemon-scented myrtle, lemon thyme and lemon-scented geranium. More unusual would be an Aniseed Garden with anise, French tarragon, aniseed myrtle and licorice.

For blind or blindfolded people, construct a path with ropes as a handrail. They can follow the ropes into an area and try to guess the plants growing there by their aroma or their feel. Make sure this is safe; I visited one such garden which featured a surprise pond and thorny bushes.

Grow aromatic plants for your bath and bathroom, such as gardenia. You may want to also grow them outside the bathroom window so their aroma wafts in.

Wild Thing

Grow bird-attracting plants near your window if you like waking up to bird-song. If you prefer to hear them later, plant them near where you eat breakfast or dinner. Plan your garden so it feeds the birds over the whole year, if you can. To attract small birds, plant bushes close together to protect them from predators such as cats. Try to have as little opening as possible for the predators to enter. It helps if the trees are spiky.

An island in a large pond provides safety for birds, reptiles and frogs. Dig cavities and plant reeds around it. This will entice them to nest. If it is too late to put in an island, then you could make a floating island on top of polystyrene, anchored in the water.

The bright purple fruit of the flax lily entice Lewin's honeyeater.

The king parrot is a bush food fanatic and loves the zigzag wattle seed even more than our bananas.

Birds are desperate for a safe niche...this rope made an appealing nest site for a scrub wren.

Place logs and branches in and around a pond and be rewarded with a delightful pageant of birds.

Establish a perch above a large pond or dam so birds can dive down to collect insects hovering above the water's surface. Birds love trees near water — especially with lateral branches. A log floating on the water is also a good place for them to dive from and they're safe from many predators.

Set up nesting boxes and sites specifically designed to attract birds and animals. They are desperate for a safe niche and will soon move in. Situate the owl box over the compost heap or pumpkin patch, so these rodent-catchers can catch mice and rats.

Get a local bird list from your council. Tick off those that visit your garden. You might like to organise the list by the season, so you can tell which ones are migratory. Allow the kids to use your binoculars, so they can join in. They might like to draw the birds on a display board and add to it over the years.

Ask the neighbours to keep their cats in at night and to ensure they have bells.

Grow plants that attract butterflies, especially rare ones. Your local Landcare group or council will be able to recommend plant species. Many of these are

The grevillea's generous flow of nectar attracts a host of birds.

plants for the larval (caterpillar) stage of the butterfly, so make sure you have a plentiful supply, as they can temporarily decimate bushes. The plant is less attractive when the caterpillars are feasting on it so plant it away from the pretty garden. Remember, without caterpillars there can be no butterflies. I heard of one lady who killed all the caterpillars on her butterfly bush because she thought they wouldn't leave anything for the butterflies.

Gourdy birds.

A Plot With Character

🌿 *Raise plants with interesting seed-vessels.* For example, the boat-like black bean shell, crow's ash seed pods in the shape of five-pointed stars, and dinosaur, bottle and one-metre long snake gourds.

🌿 *Grow plants for indoor arrangements* — flowers, foliage, branches, grasses, berries and seed cones. Try proteas and grevilleas and long-stemmed flowers such as kangaroo paws. For foliage I like the Mt Morgan silver wattle, maidenhair ferns, and kangaroo grass. Sometimes I include lilly pilly berries and acacia and hakea pods.

🌿 *A story or poem garden.* As people stroll along a pathway, a story or poem unravels. Sculptures can also line a path and tell a story.

🌿 *Make waterproof sculptures* or pictures of beneficial pest predators, such as ladybirds, dragonflies, frogs and lizards, and place them throughout the garden, so people know what to look for and nurture.

🌿 *Make models* of animal footprints and when laying cement paths stamp these into it. If the path is wide enough (like a driveway) you could even impress dinosaur footprints. Make your own cut-out or template — try your museum for dimensions. Or try creating patterns in the path by pressing leaves into the cement while it is still wet. Use large and extravagantly shaped leaves, such as those of the philodendron.

'Help me out of here …'

Make clay sculptures of each other's heads. Fire them and place them in the part of the garden each respective person enjoys most.

A sea garden — collect shells, driftwood and anything else washed up (maybe even the odd thong) to make collections, statues or collages.

Cultivate Culture

An ancient Mediterranean garden (especially suits dry areas) — showing how it would have been in biblical times — with figs, olives, grape arches, thyme, pomegranate, Lebanese cress and rock sculptures.

A bush tucker garden. Familiarise yourself with some of the native foods eaten by Aborigines. Make a bush food snack track, including small-leaved lilly pillies, macadamia nuts, midyim berries and sandpaper figs. The leaf bases of palm trees can be moulded to carry water or store fruit. Children can construct shelters from nearby materials for sleepovers.

Create an Asian garden with citrus, Vietnamese mint (in a pot), bok choi, pak choi, lotus, water chestnuts, a curry leaf tree, rice, a kaffir lime, bamboo shoots, coriander, fish plant, galangal, ginger, garlic, snake gourd, Japanese pumpkin, lemon grass, mizuna, water spinach, chilli and turmeric.

Train Your Garden to Heal

Garden beds that each treat a different illness. Lavender in a pillow and chamomile tea help with insomnia, dill and fennel seed aid digestion. For a sore throat, gargle an infusion of purple sage four times daily. An infusion of oregano in tea can help with coughs; and marjoram can be used similarly for colds.

A description next to each of the medicinal plants. Refer to them when you have problems such as:

Aloe vera — rub the gel on stings, burns and sunburn

Peppermint — make a strong tea to reduce bad breath and help indigestion

Ginger — make into tea to reduce nausea

Lemon juice — use in tea to relieve a sore throat.

Learning From Your Land

Observation is the backbone of a great garden, but do not confine your attention only to what's happening on your land. Consider the elements that come from outside: hot summer sun, welcome winter sun, wind, weeds, stormwater, soil types, noise and frost. If you know what affects your land and take this into account while designing, when the rains flood down or the windstorms thrash, you can sit back with a cup of tea and enjoy the show.

A tree fern frond about to unfurl.

*J*hree years ago, I visited an Aboriginal family who lived in the coastal monsoon belt at the top end of Australia. A necessary breeze cooled us but there were indications that at times the weather could be unforgiving. Close to their homestead there was a windmill that had once stood proud but now it lay ravaged by strong wind, casting the shadow of a mortified limbo dancer. Although the signs of these damaging winds seemed obvious, they were clearly not evident enough for a well-meaning development worker who, in good faith, had just planted an avocado tree — a plant that suffers badly if exposed to strong winds — near the windmill.

There is not a sprig of grass that shoots uninteresting to me.
Thomas Jefferson

It's enchanting to fantasise about plucking the succulent harvest of fruit trees but if the conditions don't suit, and they're neither adapted nor changed, the dream can turn into a nightmare. This chapter shows how to observe, understand and learn from the major factors that affect your garden, including those that come from beyond it. It's tempting to leap into the gardening without going through this process. Don't. People and plants will pay the price later.

Having a more in-depth feel for your garden often leads to further questions. The chapters that follow, Creating the Big Picture and Designing in Detail, will hopefully answer many of them.

Design to manage seasonal surpluses.

After months of preparation the dragon fruit flower opens with a flourish of perfumed satin...for one night only.

Drawing a Base Map

When I designed our garden seven years ago, I appreciated and imagined less than I do now. Yet, even then, clarifying the design basics helped me get started. I walked around scantily clad at night to feel the cool and warm spots of the garden (not recommended in mid-winter Tasmania). I talked with neighbours about prevailing winds and rainfall patterns, noted the sun's angles and set out to understand the land in order to work with all of its subtleties. I paid attention to things like frost, wind, pests, the brutal summer sun, rampant weeds, and even, I confess, rampant ego. I fertilised my mind's garden with Buddhist teachings on patience.

One way to learn from observation is to map graphically what exists — this is known as a Base Map. Start with a big piece of paper, a light pencil, a rubber, a ruler and a tape-measure. It helps if the paper is larger than the scaled-down property boundaries so there is room to map where the outside influences come from. Don't worry about replicating your land exactly but at least draw it roughly to scale. This is only to give you an idea. You will draw over the top of this Base Map later when you decide what you want to go in the garden. Remember to put in North. Be careful not to mislead yourself: people often draw trees too small, indicating extra space they don't have. Go through the following list of influences on your land, including those not easily seen.

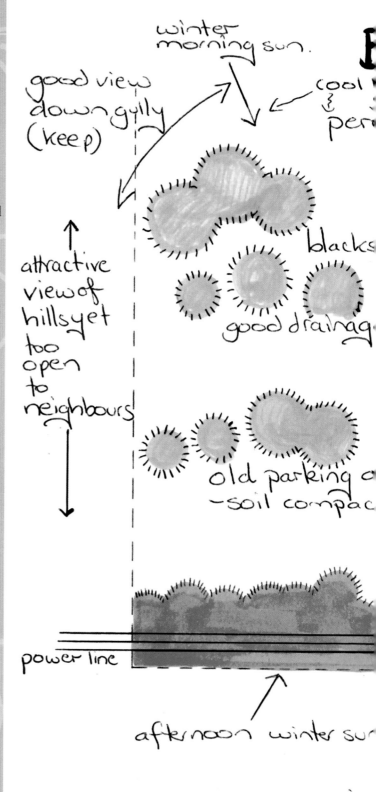

winter morning sun.

good view down gully (keep)

cool & per

attractive view of hills yet too open to neighbours

blacks

good drainag

old parking
-soil compac

power line

afternoon winter su

nois

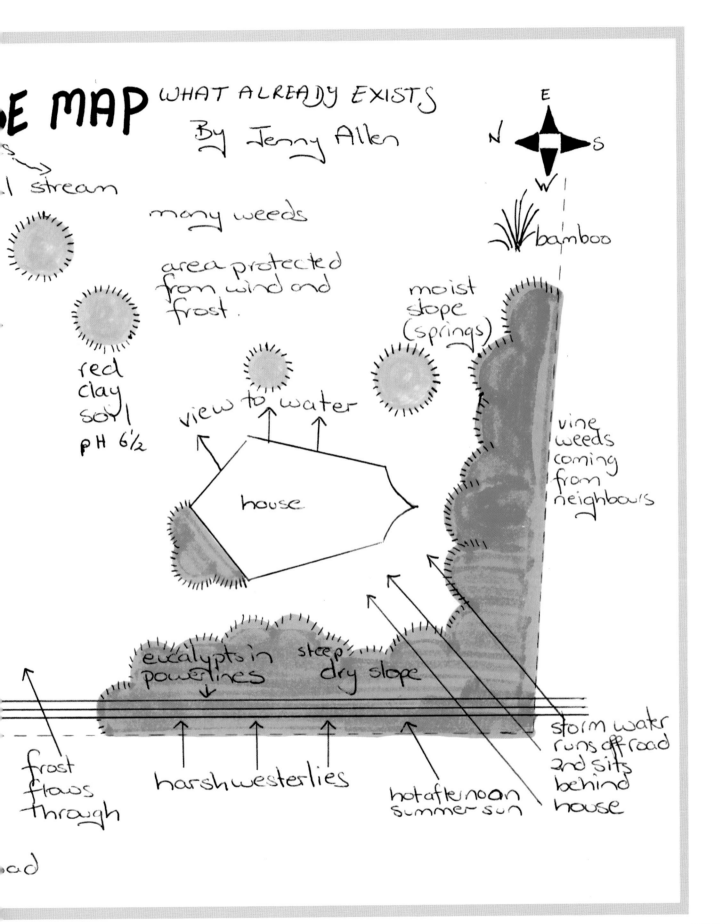

E MAP WHAT ALREADY EXISTS
By Jenny Allen

N E S W

bamboo

stream

many weeds

area protected from wind and frost.

moist slope (springs)

red clay soil pH 6½

view to water

vine weeds coming from neighbours

house

eucalypts in powerlines

steep dry slope

storm water runs off road and sits behind house

frost flows through

harsh westerlies

hot afternoon summer sun

ad

Summer and Winter Sun

S un, the energiser of plants, is a prerequisite for survival and growth. By maximising the effects of winter sun and minimising the effects of hot afternoon summer sun, the garden grows at its best.

Ascertain the daily arcs traced over your garden by winter and summer sun. Basically the winter sun follows a low arc in the sky travelling from north-east to north-west (south-east to south-west in the northern hemisphere); the summer sun is more vertical in the sky, with a wider arc rising closer to east and setting closer to west.

Walk around in the early morning, at midday and in the late afternoon. Record the angles of the sun and where it shines. If you're unable to

Let the shadows cast on hot paving advise you where to put a pergola with a deciduous vine.

Look at the shapes and shadows cast by different trees. Some skinny trees like this Davidson's plum produce very little shade.

observe this over the different seasons try to remember from past experience. Where do the shadows fall at different times of the day, especially those cast by taller structures and trees? Note the types of shadows given by umbrella-shaped trees compared to the more upright ones, such as eucalypts and Davidson's plum. Also assess the relationship between the house and the garden. Do the trees help to shield the house from summer sun blasting through its windows? Do they allow precious morning and afternoon winter sun to penetrate? Feel the heat reflected and radiated by structures at different times of the year, such as white walls and dark paving.

Add these sun and shade, winter and summer factors to your Base Map. In the next chapter you will see how to create micro-climates for different seasons, according to the sun's angle.

Of course, different people want different things. A friend of mine designed an east-facing room as his bedroom, on a hill that faces east, and didn't want to plant any shade trees. He enjoys the 4.45 a.m. shock of summer sun. It's his wake-up call and he responds by jumping out of bed. He's searching for a woman to share his routine. He's been single for a while now.

Water surfaces mirror sunlight, increasing its effect.

Wind

Australia's early settlers often lived on hilltops as it was easier to defend farmland they could see from their houses. However, life wasn't trouble-free, as many also had to endure high-velocity winds. Maybe that's why their beards were so dishevelled.

Wind-affected areas are not solely those found on hilltops. Both harmful and beneficial winds prevail on most gardens at certain times of the year. On a dry windy day, many leafy plants, even if well watered, can't drink rapidly enough to counter the water they are losing. They stop growing and often become injured before wilting. The damage can be worse than it first appears. Fruit trees take

Carambolas can handle some wind, however in the windy season we didn't irrigate this one enough and it died soon after this photo. Its protected sister is thriving.

Not as high-tech as an anemometer, the blow-away Hat Test can still tell you where you need a windbreak.

longer to show symptoms; by the time they do, they may already be severely stressed — it could be too late to revive them.

Many wind-exposed gardens rely on constant water, and if the owner wants time off from this arduous duty, forget it. Knowing this, many people over-react by establishing multiple windbreaks. However, if these are not designed carefully, they can block pleasant summer breezes.

To encourage beneficial winds and discourage harmful ones, start by monitoring them. Venture out on windy days and note the wind directions. Estimate how it affects you and the plants around you. Cultivate some empathy for your plants: if it's howling a gale and you're sitting hypnotised by a crackling fire, imagine how the plants feel with no cosy place to shelter.

Equally be aware of the refreshing breezes on a scalding day. Feel where they flow from and to. Sense if they help aerate the house and garden and ease your mind. If they do, take special care to note these, so you don't obstruct them with plants or buildings.

Nature's balmy sighs flow through a house and garden keeping it fresh and aerated, helping prevent mould growing on the walls, leather shoes and belts. My sister and her partner once rented a house in an area thickly enclosed by trees. Once, when she asked him to grab her black leather belt, he returned after five minutes replying 'I can only find a green suede one'.

Notice how the trees and structures in your area coerce the wind. Are they funnelling it or reducing it?

If you don't have time to monitor the winds in your area, then ask your neighbours or local weather station about them and examine similar locations nearby. Can you see delicate plants thriving in these open areas? Or can you see the symptoms of harsh winds, such as trees leaning to one side? If your neighbourhood is full of windbreaks, take the hint from what you see.

On your Base Map, indicate the direction of your main beneficial and harmful winds. At this stage you should take note of which winds you want to encourage, which ones you want to reduce significantly and those you are able to adapt to. Later in the book, on page 97, I discuss designing effective windbreaks and include some edible windbreak species.

Weeds

We are fortunate to have such fertile soil at our place. Our plants leap skywards, but sadly, not nearly with the same enthusiasm as our weeds. Weeds are an enormous issue in our garden—as in most—and it takes clever mapping, planning and gardening to manage them and my sanity.

Perhaps if we could penetrate Nature's secrets we should find that what we call weeds are more essential to the well-being of the world than the most precious fruit or grain.

Nathaniel Hawthorne

The pale blue fluffy-topped ageratum runs riot through the garden, and I'm inclined to treat it as a weed; in Melbourne, it sells for $8 a small bunch. A quick calculation and I find I'm a millionaire. All I need to do is borrow some big corporation's marketing and sales team for a month... I haven't found another use for the ageratum (although apparently its chewed up heads can be used on tick bites to reduce swelling and irritation).

If you are lucky, you may not feel the weeds in your garden are serious enough to map on your Base Map. Their potential harm is not always easy to assess, as the two conflicting quotes in this section signify. If, however, you have invasive weeds you probably require some serious weed management. It's a good idea to indicate the worst-affected areas on your map. This way you will remember it is an important element in your garden that needs consideration.

The quality for which weeds are most renowned is persistence. Start by identifying the ones that do the most damage in the garden. Ask your local council or Landcare group for a list of invasive local weeds. Among the worst are vigorous plants that ruin the lives of plants nearby, vines that climb up and strangle trees, plants which spread easily by seed as well as those that spread vigorously in both sun and shade; also plants that reshoot in many places after being cut, take over grass and pastureland and irritating plants with prickly or sticky seeds.

Although these weeds are the ones you probably don't want to know about, dealing with them first up could save you over ten or even one hundred times more work down the track. One of my father's favourite sayings is 'A stitch in time saves nine...'

Some weeds you may agree to tolerate or put

The fluffy blue top: the South pay big dollars for them —— the North pay big dollars for them to be obliterated.

The threats from introduced pests are certainly more immediate than the risk of military attack.

Ian Lowe, New Scientist 1997

on a waiting list for elective surgery, addressing them later down the track. Low-spreading weeds are bearable in a confined area if they don't spread by seeds, are not too competitive and won't strangle the plants amongst them.

Stormwater

Stormwater can leave ugly scars over the landscape and throughout the bank account. So don't wait until storms loom on the horizon — assume they will, prepare ahead and when they thunder over, relax and relish the lightning show.

Venture out in a heavy downpour and watch where the water flows.

To begin preparations, walk outside with a big umbrella on a day of heavy rain. Look at the different directions the water is running. The vulnerable spots in the garden will become evident — typically places that collect a lot of water and can't manage it. This water often comes from a large catchment or a hard, steep surface where it runs off quickly. Check for any signs of erosion and water damage. Especially watch out for water banking up behind the house or going underneath it, as it can cause rising damp and may even shift the foundations.

When the rain stops, draw the water-flows through your garden; you will then be in a better position to deploy a water management strategy. At our place we initially had some fairly major stormwater problems but we applied some water management principles and developed a Water Management Plan. To read more about these, turn to page 105 and page 119 respectively.

The rhythm suddenly changes; the rain stops and diamond droplets sparkle as sunbeams dance.

Soil Types

You probably have various soil types throughout your garden. By recognising what is where you can plant trees in the soil of their preference, and consequently spend less on fertiliser, lime and water.

The stunning cinnamon tree is related to the avocado, and like it, it prefers light, well-drained soil. To make cinnamon quills, the branches of the tree are pruned and the bark cut off.

Dig up different patches of soil and feel for differences in moisture level, temperature and texture. Do they feel sandy, loamy or clay-like? To tell if the soil has a high clay content, mix it with a little water and see if it can be rolled into a smooth sausage that is often cohesive enough to

mould a bracelet. Sandy soil has much larger particles and doesn't hold together. Good quality loam is made up of a lot of air space, water, silt/sand, clay, humus and organic matter. If loam is mixed with a bit of water and compressed it will only just hold together.

Gardening without knowing whether your soil is acid or alkaline (pH level) can be like gardening in the dark with your sunglasses on. Often there are nutrients in the garden that plants can't absorb because of their soil pH. To find out how acid or alkaline your soil is, buy a pH test kit. These are sold cheaply at gardening stores. By determining your soil pH, you can work out which plants suit the existing conditions or what you need to balance the soil for the plants you want to grow.

Cracks in dry soil indicate a high clay content.

Looking at the condition and colour of a stressed-looking plant can also tell you a lot about deficiencies in the soil. A leaf analysis chart can help identify which micro- or macro-nutrients your plants may be missing. These charts can be obtained from many fertiliser companies and government agriculture departments. If you are serious or notice plants are not growing well you can also have a professional soil analysis done.

It is best to determine the different soil textures and pH readings from a whole range of sections from the garden. To find out more about how to modify or improve your soil, turn to pages 107 and 202.

Noise

A friend of a friend wanted to test the different sounds that an average person unconsciously endures. He played Beethoven over his loudspeakers, belting it out over the neighbourhood. The complaints came thick and fast. Then he recorded the sound of a lawn mower and belted this out over the neighbourhood at the same noise level. No one complained. If aliens from outer space wanted to take over they would simply have to imitate lawn mowers and no one would question a thing.

Before planning be mindful that beautiful displays of birds can come with a soundtrack.

Different noises affect us in unpredictable ways. I loathe to be disturbed when concentrating and so I sometimes wear tractor muffs while I write. This also tends to scare people off. Either way it's more peaceful, so the muffs are a win-win situation for me.

Identify the noises that affect you while in the garden. From what source and direction do they emanate? What time of day do they mostly occur and how predictable are these noises? Do other people hear them too, or is it only you? How bearable are they?

There may also be particular noises you want to keep, such as the morning chimes of bellbirds. Mark any favourable or unfavourable noises on your base map. On page 110 we look at ways in which to use nature and design as your volume control.

Frost

$\mathcal{F}$rost can severely damage a garden — it only takes one morning. Cold air flows like treacle over an upside-down cake — downwards to the lowest point it can find. If there's a wall or a thick clump of trees preventing it flowing under, it will bank up behind obstructions or, if possible, scroll around them. When it can flow no longer it will puddle and often creates frost. This is where it has the harshest effect. If your land is flat, frost is more likely to settle where there are no trees.

After a starry night, sneak out before the sun rises. Crystals of dew will tell you where your frosty hollows lie.

To understand the frost patterns in your area, wait until winter and monitor where it forms. Or, go out on a winter's night with only a few clothes on and feel the chilliest spots. If this seems a bit much — or a bit little — then you could buy a minimum/maximum thermometer and take readings from different spots over the season.

If you don't have the time for this kind of close monitoring then talk it over with your neighbours and old-timers. Keep an eye out for indicators: are frost-susceptible perennials thriving nearby on similar terrain or are all the plants frost tolerant?

Although frost may come as a surprise, much of it is predictable. In many instances the impact of frost can be significantly diluted, even eliminated. I once worked on a property where a Frost Diversion Arc had been grown uphill from the garden (see page 112). It survived the inevitable severe frost, while surrounding gardens were wiped out: a success story due to the owner's monitoring, anticipation and careful planning.

Evaluate specific micro-climates on your land, especially if you want to push the limits like we do with pawpaws. To protect them from frost they are planted downhill from the house and around the dam.

Remember, frost doesn't always have a negative impact. It can assist the garden as well, sweetening fruits, helping flower buds mature and knocking back many weeds and pests.

Creating the Big *Picture*

Address the root causes of potential problems instead of continually combating their symptoms. Better to plan a garden carefully than to go charging outside with an artillery of machetes and sprays, fighting a battle that can never be won. Design for a peaceful garden that works for you — one that helps create beneficial micro-climates, improves the soil, reduces harmful wind, creates pleasant breezes and keeps weeds at bay.

Orange poppy.

Often gardening is reduced to pure aesthetics. People think that blues and mauves look nice together, that climbing sweet peas will form a dramatic backdrop to a bed of petunias. But imagine if car manufacturers thought this way: that aesthetic appeal was the most important thing…even in your favourite colour, a car that doesn't go makes no sense. Designing is a merging of aesthetic and practical considerations. At the heart of every great garden is forethought; lack of it will create a real headache.

Plan for the future … that is where you are going to spend the rest of your life. Mark Twain

Attack of the Innocent Seedling.

What's the connection between a twenty-first century bank and a lofty eucalypt? They both drop their branches. An unplanned garden can be as perilous as a large tree swaying dangerously above the house on a stormy night, or as vampish as a pine tree sapping the life out of nearby fruit trees. In an unplanned garden the vegie patch is too far from the house and so lies abandoned, grass chokes young trees, pests rampage, the dry winds howl through, precious nutrients and water leach away and the giant fig tree cracks the neighbour's house foundations. Weekends are spent pumping the spray gun, behind the mower, or terrorising the neighbours with the whipper-snipper. When the garden is planned badly it becomes like Frankenstein's monster because the creator and victim are one.

Good design is not just a theoretical abstract but rather an ongoing creative act that guides gardeners to a productive and imaginative use of space. It can be challenging, but not for long.

A different perspective gained from a tree or rooftop can give valuable design insights.

Trees are an intergenerational investment so choose your portfolio wisely. They can pay handsome dividends in shelter, food and as habitat for plants and animals. They mine nutrients from the soil and water from aquifers.

A well-designed garden is gentle on the wallet. It becomes the apple of your eye, not the melon of your colic. It triggers a rich variety of sensuous responses, offering greener avenues and healthier banquets for the imagination to explore. A productive and beautiful garden is not just a collection of plants but an integrated community within which you have a sense of place. It supplies so many of your culinary, creative and cultural requirements and it does the bulk of the work for you, the natural way.

Nature is too powerful to ever lose. So, take a walk on the wild side and encourage nature to play a bigger role. Replicate natural cycles and systems so the garden can power ahead. You can take a holiday — for short periods — knowing the garden can be left in charge and your homecoming will be a celebration of pleasant surprises.

Grape expectations — easily satisfied.

Above: Show-off foliage loves an audience. We booked early for a gallery seat to see the flaming whorls of the Davidson's plum planted below our verandah.
Right: Davidson's plums ripe for making jam and cordial.

This chapter is about the big picture. It's tempting to jump into the familiar territory of hands-on gardening solutions. Hold off for the moment — these are detailed later. Contemplate your design a little while longer. Take time out to consider possible ways to ameliorate some of the less desirable influences and harness the desirable ones.

Each of the areas covered in the previous chapter is considered again here, but this time the emphasis is on solutions. Before drawing up a Concept Design, run through the 18-Point Design Checklist that follows. This will help concentrate your mind on important issues to think about at this stage.

Some people find it easier to take advice about their love life or raising their children than they do about their garden. Throw off your shackles.

Remember how good it felt? If not, try it now.

Obstacles are those frightful things you see when you take your eyes off the goal.

Anon

Have friends around to talk over your design. Visit other gardens, talk to the owners if possible, and participate in local groups and courses. Ask lots of questions and don't be scared of how you sound. There is only one stupid question — the one you don't ask.

Try to involve the family from the design stage onwards. They may want to take responsibility for different sections. If you are designing well, you will be minimising overwhelming maintenance. At the same time, dare to be different, interesting and exciting. An ideal solution to any problem is one that not only looks beautiful but one that works well.

Your Eden is about to spring forth. Obstacles will arise, so make a commitment to work through them. Remember to relish the learning experiences, to smell the roses (and the pennyroyal, the kaffir lime leaves, etc.). Gardening this way can be a fulfilling experience and you'll learn about yourself as you navigate your way through the decision-making process. Relax in the knowledge that this is a step-by-step process; it doesn't all need to happen now. I suggest taking photos in the early stages. The changes you will see down the garden path may astound you.

18-Point Design Checklist

1. How can you make the garden low maintenance?
2. How much time, energy and enthusiasm can you muster?
3. What food do you and your family want and how much?

4. What beneficial micro-climates can you create?
5. How can you entice cool summer breezes but deflect harmful wind?
6. How can you shade summer afternoon sun yet optimise winter sun?
7. Is there a view to enhance or block out?
8. Do you need to screen noisy neighbours?
9. Do you need to respect neighbours' winter sun or view?
10. Is frost a problem? If so how can you reduce it?

11. What plants and structures do you want?
12. What does each plant require?
13. What is the mature height and width of each major tree you're planning for?
14. How will the garden evolve over time — spacing/sunlight needs/production?

15. What are your soil variations in different areas — texture, critical deficiencies, acid or alkaline?
16. How can you optimise water use — disperse it, keep it on high ground, plant appropriately?
17. How can you quickly drain excess stormwater?

18. Can you incorporate the 10 Permaculture Principles, along with some lateral thinking, into your design?

Concept Design

A Concept Design addresses the root causes of some of the problems you envisage may arise from the internal and external influences on your garden. It is applicable to a new garden or to upgrade an existing one. If appropriate, this can be drawn on top of your Base Map. Or you may want to put tracing paper over your Base Map and draw on this.

On the right is the Concept Design I did for our place. It shows where things should be but doesn't go into detail at this stage. For example, I planned for a Bush Food Snack Track but didn't stipulate specific species. These come later in a Detailed Design (see page 118).

If you're more physical and prefer modelling, try crafting a Concept Design. You could use clay, Plasticine, cardboard cut-outs, Fuzzy Felt stick-ons, papier-mâché or moist sand. The props are all around you: small branches with leaves on them for trees, sticks for boundaries, and rocks for dwellings.

The rest of the chapter highlights what to think about for a Concept Design, so you might like to read through it before starting to map things out. At times designing can be hard work but, as the pieces of the puzzle come together and the big picture starts to emerge, it can feel exhilarating.

My Concept Design is not exactly to scale or precise — more impressionistic. Conveying the essence is more important at this stage. I have drawn the boundary of the land in dots rather than a heavy line. This is so I remember, and can sometimes draw, those things that are outside the boundary that affect it.

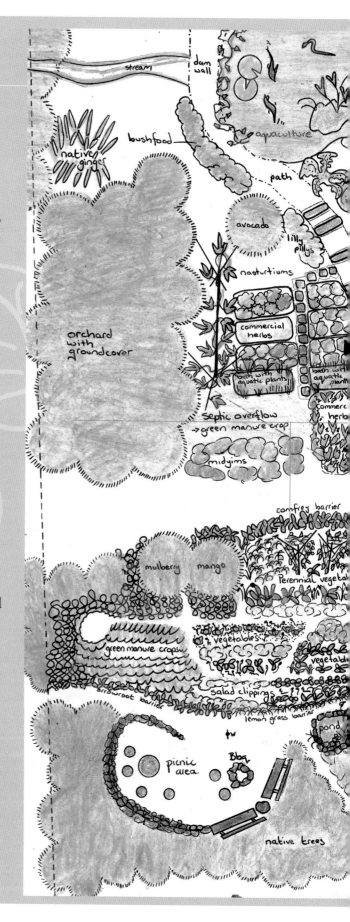

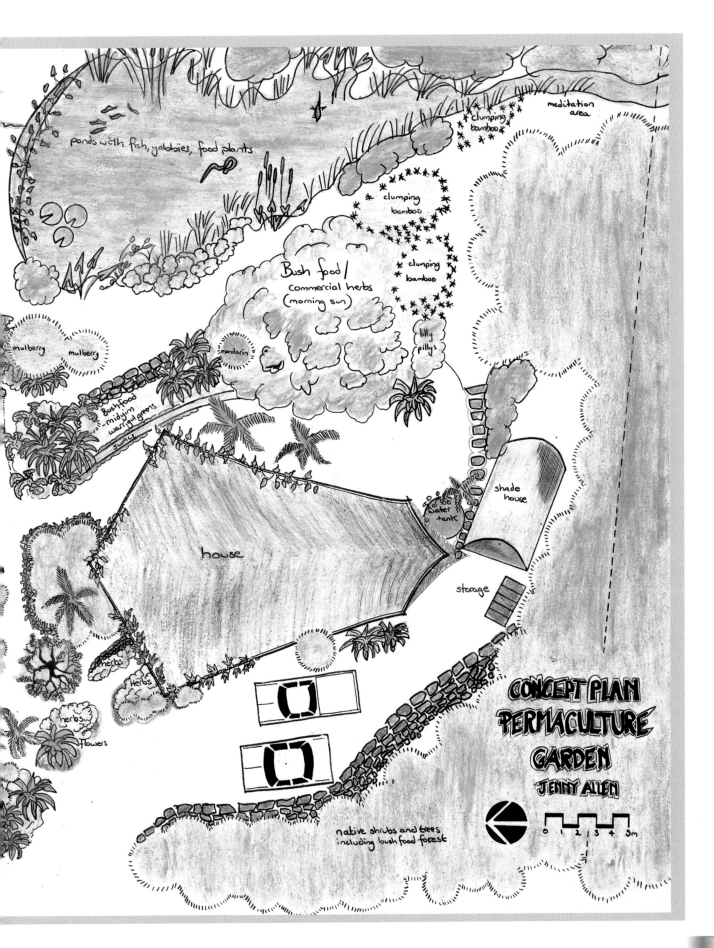

ponds with fish, yabbies, food plants

meditation area

clumping bamboo

clumping bamboo

clumping bamboo

Bush food /
commercial herbs
(morning sun)

lilly pillys

mulberry   mulberry

mandarin

Bush food
midjim
warrigul greens
swale

shade house

water tanks

house

storage

herbs

Herbs

herbs

flowers

CONCEPT PLAN
PERMACULTURE
GARDEN
JENNY ALLEN

0 1 2 3 4 5m

native shrubs and trees
including bush food forest

Creating Beneficial Micro-climates

S un on the back in winter; cool breezes and shade in summer; fresh tropical fruits in cooler areas — these are some of the joys of micro-climates. Micro-climates are localised conditions distinctive to an area — they are either natural or made by humans. By maximising existing ones or producing new ones you can extend the range of food you grow. They also extend the amount of comfortable time in your garden — both in summer and winter.

The classic sun trap — the palms thrive on the southern side of the dam because the winter sun reflects off the water and onto them.

Maximising Winter Sun

Try to encourage the winter morning, midday and afternoon sun to flow into your garden and house, not blocking it at any stage. Place large items that cast long shadows on the southerly side, although be careful not to shade out your neighbour — a huge shadow can be a real dampener for neighbourly relations.

Grow sun-loving plants on a north-facing slope so they receive as much sun as possible through winter. On the northern and eastern side of your garden plant only small trees or bushes, and deciduous trees. Note when the deciduous trees spring into leaf; some regain their leaves in early spring, blocking out valuable sun when it is still low in the sky.

Also grow plants that need a lot of warmth on the northern side of walls, rocks or taller plants. Light-coloured structures reflect extra heat during the day and dark ones collect heat and emit it throughout the night. These structures also block wind, increase humidity and their thermal mass decreases the chances of frost. Whatever the property's aspect, these tactics can be employed to increase the warmth; however, it is most effective if the property is facing north.

Water tends to hold heat, so place plants that like the most warmth on the southern side of a dam or body of water. The winter sun will not only shine onto the plants but also reflect from the water onto them — increasing their sunbath. The water also warms the area at night, decreasing the chance of frost.

Grow warm-loving plants in pots and take them into a sunny spot in the house or greenhouse in winter.

We use the range of micro-climates around the house to grow plants not normally adapted to our climatic zone.

A solid vertical structure that faces the sun can store and reflect heat, especially during the critical winter period.

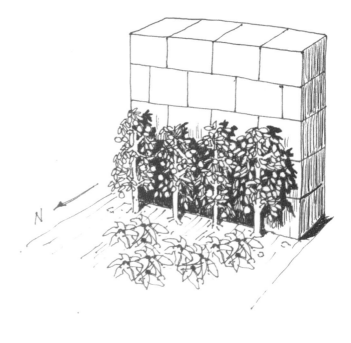

N

Try to plan sitting areas to be open to the north. Impromptu winter picnics can make the most of a burst of sunshine. Also have a sunny flat area for warm afternoon naps. A vertical background, such as a white wall or a tree with pale leaves, will reflect still more heat. Maybe have an earthen amphitheatre that faces north.

Have a kids' play area open to the north-west so after school in winter they can frolic in the last remnants of sun.

The self-seeding bok choi is more productive where it is shaded from the midday summer sun by the corn.

Grow your own sunscreen — multiple layers of plants. The overlapping banana and cocoyam leaves create a more temperate micro-climate, minimising the effects of hot sun.

Minimising Summer Sun

To cut out hot afternoon sun, plant lots of umbrella-shaped shade trees, especially to the west and overhead. Many layers of plants also create a cooler micro-climate and maintain soil moisture for longer.

Plan a number of cool shady areas in the garden in which to work and play at different times of the day. These shady areas could be half outside and half inside, like verandahs and pergolas. A splashing fountain near a cool sitting area adds to a sense of wellbeing on a hot summer's afternoon.

For ease of movement, construct shaded walkways that link these areas. Make cool, soft paths from bark chips, small beach pebbles or grass so you can walk comfortably in bare feet.

In summer the vegetable garden and heat-intolerant species prefer the morning sun and by mid-afternoon are happy to be partly shaded. If possible plan the vegie garden to face north-east. If you don't have a slope, grow deciduous large trees to the west — although not so close that they steal water and nutrients.

Designing Effective Windbreaks

*I*n a frantic attempt to control blasting winds it's tempting to create the ultimate windbreak that prevents the least whisper flowing through. This can do more harm than good. When the wind flows over the windbreak it curls over and plunges down the other side like a wave. Here it creates distinctive turbulence. Paradoxically, this is where protection is needed most.

To prevent this, allow about 40% of wind to flow through the windbreak (the windbreak should be slightly see-through when mature). If there's enough room, plant it three trees thick. The windbreak should be as long as possible and at a right angle to the prevailing winds. The height of the windbreak influences over what distance it will remain effective. According to Bill Mollison in his book *Introduction to Permaculture*, a windbreak can reduce wind on the leeward side — that is the side protected from the wind — by up to 30 times its height. For example, if your windbreak features trees that are 5 metres high, it will offer protection from wind for up to 150 metres.

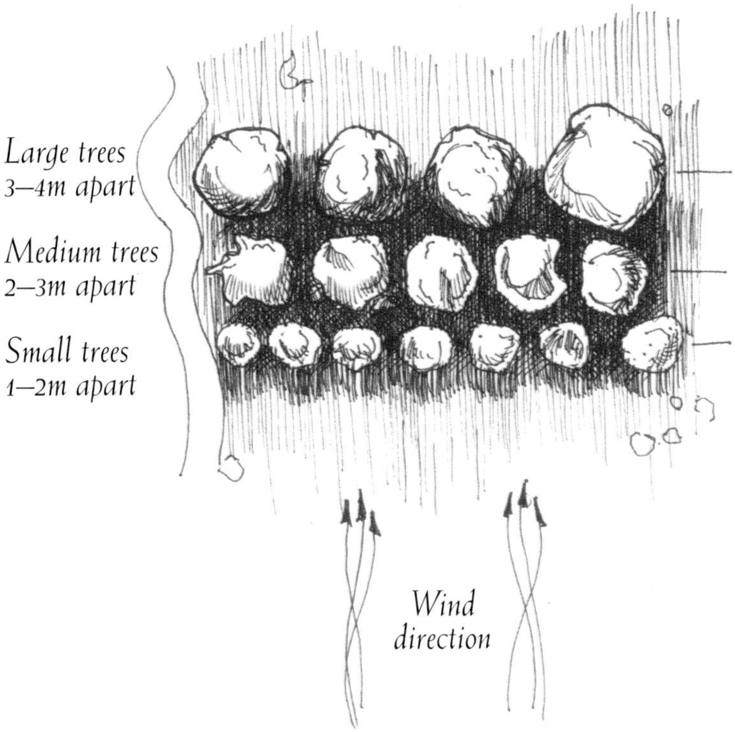

Windbreaks need to be adapted to each particular situation. The template shown here is a starting point. The smallest trees are the front-line to the wind and the higher trees are at the back. Plant according to their mature width.

Large trees
3–4m apart

Medium trees
2–3m apart

Small trees
1–2m apart

Wind
direction

Effective Windbreak

Windbreak allows 40% of wind through trees

Little turbulence

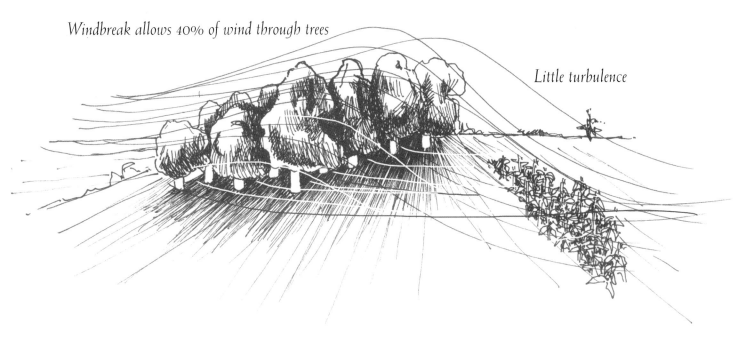

Ineffective Windbreak

Wind deflected over dense windbreak

Damaging turbulence

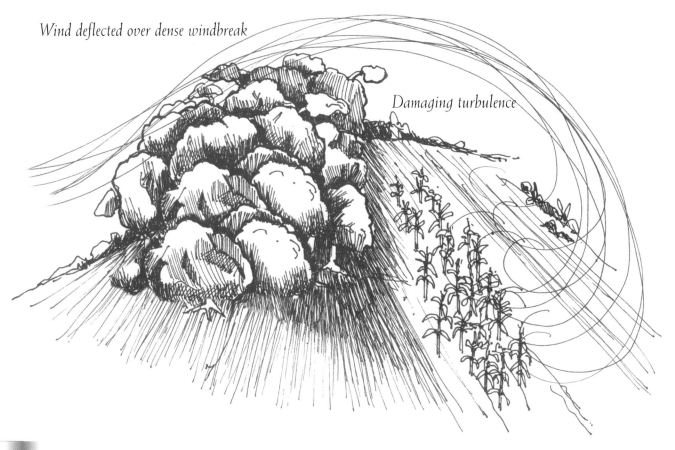

Windbreak Features

Successful windbreak trees are resilient; they flow with the blows, rather than being brittle and breaking. They block the wind for the entire height of the tree; in other words, the limbs start near the bottom of the tree and spread evenly throughout. Some of the lines of cypresses around Victoria that have been employed as windbreaks have a great yawning gap below the lowest limbs and the ground. The air rushes through these gaps, producing wind tunnels.

Windbreak trees are often a mixture of fast-growing, short-lived species, such as acacias, interspersed among slower growing long-lived species. This means the windbreak starts to be effective earlier. When the short-lived ones die out, the slower ones take over. If the vegetable garden needs protection from the wind, it's best to plant smaller species so their roots don't invade.

Breaking wind does not have to be the windbreak's only function. They may also: block noise and nosey neighbours; be ornamental, such as grevilleas and Mt Morgan silver wattle; provide cut flowers and foliage for the house; and be pruned in the non-windy season to create mulch. We use the native mulberry — *Pipturus argenteus* — for mulch. It's a wind-resistant tree, yet it also tolerates us snapping off its many thin branches and grows back vigorously.

Unlike smooth-trunked eucalypts, plants like this lilly pilly retain their lower limbs, making them better windbreaks.

Fruit Trees That Can Make Good Windbreaks

The following trees can be used in windbreaks providing the wind is not too severe. Expect a reduction in fruit and, if necessary, give the trees more water than otherwise as the wind dries them out. Young trees may need to be protected. If possible, select fruit trees that are not flowering or fruiting when the wind is predicted to be harshest.

Black mulberry	Olive
Carob	Pine nut
Feijoa	Red cherry guava
Jaboticaba	Rose apple
Longan	White sapote
Loquat	Yellow cherry guava
Mango	

Weed Management Plan

Keeping the garden weed-free can be like painting the Sydney Harbour Bridge — when it's finally finished, that's the time to start all over again. So design to make the work less repetitive. The best defence is to make growth conditions for weeds as unfavourable as possible and to manage weeds as soon as they appear.

Look for plants like this peppermint-scented geranium that can be spread easily from cuttings and smother weeds.

In both these points, mulch is a great ally. Mulch helps to invigorate the soil, stimulating the growth of the plants you want, which if adequately provided for and placed strategically, will eventually out-compete weeds. At the same time it can be used to smother weeds, starving them of sunlight and nutrients. Remember the design principle of Multiple Uses on page 32? Mulch is this permaculture principle in action.

So when you're planning your garden, design with mulch in mind. How large is the area you need to mulch? Are you able to grow your own mulch, such as arrowroot, comfrey and lemon grass? Regular mulching can be hard work and expensive, so plan your garden with these restrictions in mind. Know the amount of mulch you can afford, how much cardboard and newspaper you can access and how much time you have.

Use the Zoning Principle and mulch the areas closest to the house the most intensively. Then, as you fan out from the house, create mulch islands for groups of plants. Further out, spot-mulch trees as they are usually distributed more sparsely and are larger. When plants are young and small, it is vital to mulch them. Once trees are large enough they create sufficient shade to reduce grass and weed invasion by themselves. Only then is it not so necessary to mulch.

To eventually reduce the need to mulch, grow dense groundcovers between trees, such as blue eye and peppermint geranium. There are also a wide range of edible groundcovers, such as pepino, midyim berry and Warrigal greens. Each of these can survive full sun and also handles the transition to dappled shade when the trees grow. Cover crops — perennial carpets of long-term plants such as alfalfa and white clover — also out-compete weeds.

I divided one dense native blue eye and strategically placed cuttings throughout the garden where it now out-competes weeds. As the trees grow larger, blue eye handles the transition from full sun to dappled shade.

Beneficial hoverflies and blue-banded native bees are seduced by the blue eye's cheeky wink.

To keep the weeds out of the orchard we employ a zesty hippy with a floral shirt — Nas Turtium.

Plan for there to be few gaps between trees, bushes and groundcovers when maximum plant growth is achieved — then there's less chance for grass and weeds to catch the sun, space and nutrients they need for a takeover bid. To achieve this, design with the foreknowledge of the plants' mature shapes and how long it will take them to reach full size. Determine which weeds die from being partially shaded and which ones soldier on. Don't assume all plants will handle this transition — many don't and when they eventually die, shade-loving weeds take over.

To begin the process of eliminating weeds and grass, first mulch over them and plant both fast-growing short-term plants and slower growing long-term plants among the weeds or grass. The fast-growing plants, such as nasturtiums,

pumpkins, choko and nitrogen-fixing bushes, will smother the area while the long-termers eventually establish a canopy that will deny most weeds the light they need to thrive.

Design the weed- and grass-free areas to be in blocks, rather than thin lines. This means less edge is exposed to infiltration. A garden edge often receives run-off nutrients and water, making it a prime spot for weeds. Protect edges with vigorous, non-rampant plants that enjoy the same growth conditions, inhibiting weed invasion. Lemon grass works well and it can also be continually cut back for mulch, cups of tea, Thai curries and aromatic hula skirts.

Nasturtiums as groundcovers supposedly help repel borers. Their flowers and leaves pep up a salad.

The choko is an edible groundcover but watch out as it aspires to greater heights. This social climber needs to be regularly pulled out of trees, or grow it where it will be vertically challenged, with no penthouse suite in sight.

Water Management

When I bought this fantastic house, it had one drawback: it not only looked like a boat but was actually leaning slightly to one side like a yacht in a breeze. Poor compaction and moisture beneath one of the poles had caused one side to sink 10 centimetres.

Water is the driving force of all nature. Leonardo da Vinci

The engineering consultant told me I needed to jack up the pole and put a dead man underneath. After a minute's shock and wondering whether he was going to volunteer and go quietly, he explained that 'dead man' was an engineering term for a block of wood laid horizontally.

If the water was to continue to saturate the ground under that side of the house it would take a lot of dead men to keep it afloat. Come summertime, our karma wouldn't be the only thing getting a bit whiffy.

To keep water away from the house and to safely spread stormwater and other moisture throughout the whole garden we designed a detailed Water Management Plan that can be seen on page 119. It means that our garden is more predictable so we can go on holidays knowing that it will be robust in hot weather and that the house will not break from its moorings in stormy weather. The plan is based on the following Water Principles.

Our house looks like a boat and felt like one until we diverted the water that flowed underneath it.

Water Principles

Australia, being a land of extremes, undergoes periods of flooding as well as drought. It's tricky designing to keep water in the garden while simultaneously planning for its smooth escape if there's too much, but it's worth the trouble.

Address water problems as close to their original source as possible. Like many problems, the longer they continue, the more irrevocably they impact. Assume there will be stormwater and manage it as high up as possible rather than lower down where there is more of it running faster and with fewer places to go. Look especially for hard and steep areas where the stormwater will run faster and its impact will be greater. If you get too much water run-off from the neighbours, talk to them about solutions; they may have the space to benefit from it themselves.

Try not to let too much water run quickly through your garden and away. The cheapest way to store water is in the soil. Swales, terraces and diversion drains intercept the flow of water and spread it — so it seeps into the ground in designated places rather than running over it. Swales, and how to make them, are described on page 232.

If water must converge, then send it to fruit trees that can cope with it. Among the fruit trees that can handle occasional flooding are black mulberry, hazelnut, Japanese raisin tree, lychee, mango, pecan, quince and star apple.

Before water evaporates, seeps or flows away, use it in as many ways as possible. If you are able to contain water on site, make the most of it — grow plants such as water chestnuts and lotus in ponds. In

Fruit Trees That Handle Dry Periods

Quite a lot of mature fruit trees can withstand dry periods but they need enough water until they have established themselves.

Almond	Longan
Black mulberry	Loquat
Carob	Mango
Japanese raisin tree	Olive
Date	Pine nut
Feijoa	Pistachio
Fig	Pomegranate
Granadilla	Red cherry guava
Grape	Rose apple
Grumichama	White sapote
Guava	Yellow cherry guava

boggy sites grow kangkong. If you have young children, don't forget to fence ponds and boggy areas — they could fall in or get caught in the mud.

If possible, re-use and cleanse grey-water from the bathroom and kitchen by irrigating plants with it but keep it away from the vegie garden in case it spreads pathogens onto root or leaf crops. Check with your council for regulations regarding grey-water before using it.

If you know your moist and dry areas, you can plant and water accordingly. For example, in dry areas grow lots of perennials, natives and other plants with a low water requirement. To help keep moisture in the soil and increase humidity, shade the ground by growing many layers of plants.

Strategic plantings of many sorts can cut out the hot summer afternoon sun and allow in the more gentle morning sun and some windbreaks can double up as shade.

A Fruitful Relationship

Fruit trees and other edible perennials are important in permaculture because they provide a long-term food source. They are less work than annuals and yield more. Some, like olives, can produce for over 1000 years so plan for them early as part of the Big Picture. In your Concept Plan, design for their needs to be met naturally.

Soil Management Plan

The answer to most soil problems is to simply chant OMMMMM… that's short for Organic Matter. OM can help: wet soil to drain; dry soil to retain moisture; clay soil to break up; sandy soil to become more absorbent; cold soil to warm up; warm soil to cool down; low-nutrient soil to retain nutrients and compacted soil to hold air.

Compost boosts your soil life. It introduces and feeds millions of creatures that convert minerals locked within soil particles into valuable micro-nutrients. It makes macro-nutrients available to plants and helps kill plant pathogens and nematodes.

OM is to plants what a healthy diet is to humans. It's not unknown for sick people to go out to buy vitamins to fix themselves and on the way home stop off for junk food. They'd be better off continually eating well to start with. Similarly, it's better for plants to have consistently healthy soil with a range of nutrients, rather than a fertiliser fix every now and then.

Pick up a handful of healthy soil. You are holding more living organisms than there are people on this Earth. It's squirming with life — worms, beetles, ants, bacteria, fungi — and they're ravenous. They eat each other, as well as dead organic material like leaf litter, compost, old roots, hay, mulch and dead insect bodies. They convert these into very useful humus.

A sense of humus is what the plants want. Humus is a complex material that contains moderate amounts of nutrients. More importantly, it has large stable molecules with ion-exchange sites. Like a magnet, negative ions entice and then catch positively charged ions such as potassium, iron, calcium, copper and ammonium (which contains nitrogen). The humus stores these ions so they aren't lost to the air or leached away in water. The microbes then break them off and they are free for plants to take up.

The humus also glues particles together making it easier for water and air to penetrate between them. Less soil is lost by wind or water erosion.

Overall, it's an incredibly complex biotech system, but a simple way to look at it is: the organic material is food for the micro-organisms. The micro-organisms make humus. The humus increases the availability of nutrients to the plants. To begin this cycle in the garden, design ways to have a continual supply of organic material.

Design to Increase the OM in Your Soil

Many people are aware of how to put more OM into the soil, yet few actually plan for strategies in the design stage to make this easier and more effective.

Plan for nitrogen-producing trees and bushes throughout the property, such as tagasaste and pigeon pea (beware of rampancy). Micro-organisms need nitrogen to break down carbon — they dine before the plants and will take it out of the plant's larder if it's not available elsewhere.

Multiple layers of plants with multiple layers of roots break up the soil; as the roots continually die off they provide food for micro-organisms and leave channels for water and air to enter.

Protect the garden from extreme elements — such as drought, wind and flood. They can send the soil-life packing. In boggy areas make a pond and grow aquatic species.

Put the compost heap at the top of the garden so that when it leaches the garden benefits. Another way to catch nutrients is to recycle grey-water onto ornamental plants and fruit trees.

To minimise soil compaction, design a network of pathways that reduce foot passage over the garden. Place whatever you harvest most frequently at the front of your garden beds and those used less often further back.

Grow plants to use as mulch, such as comfrey, arrowroot, lemongrass, bananas and bushes whose branches come off easily and re-shoot at many points. Mulch heavily or grow cover crops (page 231) and green manure crops (see page 229).

If planning to use plastic compost bins, have two or more so you can spread the load. A single bin can go sour if fed too much as it can't break down a family's waste fast enough.

The Biolytix Filter

We once had a compost pile and smelly septic tank — now Dean has converted it to a Biolytix Filter. It looks like a compost bin on top of the septic but in reality it is a cunningly designed organic waste and water treatment system. We simply empty all our vegetable scraps and paper into its top bin while the grey-water and sewage go into the tank below. It uses natural ecological processes, including worms and other organisms, to quickly break all this down, without odour. Voila! Instant, liquid organic fertiliser spreads through underground irrigation to selected fruit trees.

Now I can have a big bath without guilt and pull the plug knowing the water won't be wasted, or pollute the river nearby. Instead it's working hard, helping to break down organic matter, spreading nutrients safely and irrigating effectively.

Dean spent seven years inventing the Biolytix Filter. Ironically, my grandfather helped pioneer centralised sewerage systems in Australia. Dean's changing the tide and is pioneering *decentralised* systems both here and internationally. He started by studying organic matter breaking down aerobically — in cow pats and on stream edges. It was just too fascinating and he couldn't stop. During our first romantic holiday, on Fraser Island, we scrutinised worm species in septic tanks.

On our second and nearly ultimate holiday, on another idyllic island, he spent two hours in tanks half full of sewage.

It may have been worth it. A recent independent engineering study shows it's 50% cheaper for towns to install Biolytix Biowater Network Filters than conventional sewerage. The positive environmental impacts are also enormous: it minimises water use, improves the soil, decreases landfill wastes and reduces greenhouse gases. Eventually it may not only replace septic systems but conventional sewerage as well.

South Africa has bought into this Australian invention and is installing it in many sites on a larger scale, including the Ritz Carlton Hotel in Stellenbosch, nature reserves and a major conference centre. The updated Biolytix Filter was launched in Australia in October 2002. I hope Australia embraces its own home-grown product.

Designing to Reduce Annoying Noises

Both internal and external noises can make or break the enjoyment of a garden. Fortunately many can be designed away. Here are a few examples.

Frogs have different sleeping patterns to humans and flirt raucously. I know two families who filled in their pond as it was too close to their bedroom window.

Where possible, plant or build noise barriers, such as dense bushes, thick walls or long, high mounds of soil (berms). These could also double as garden accessories — the bushes and walls covered with passionfruit vine and the berms studded with plants that need well-drained soil, such as avocados and babacos.

Determine what time of day the noises are loudest and design your garden so you can avoid these. For example, if peak-hour traffic or daytime industrial noise is a problem, then make a morning breakfast nook that catches the day's first sunshine so you can enjoy a peaceful breakfast. This can also serve as an evening garden, with lights and lanterns.

Keep frog ponds away from the bedroom window or verandah. Their choruses can be deafening if too close.

Have less lawn and, therefore, less mowing noise. Less-used grassy parts of the garden may only need cutting every second time.

Create a quiet nook in your garden for secluded moments, a place of peace away from the children. This could be a sunken garden.

Eat the noisy rooster.

Frost Management Plan

rost can burn the unprepared. Yet it tends to be fairly predictable and can be transformed into an ally. If you have planned carefully, those nights you smell the frost in the air and the stars wink at you, you can wink back and go to sleep knowing all will be well.

Some fruit trees need cool conditions to induce flowering, like this apple.

Grow only frost-tolerant plants in frost-prone areas. Especially those that have a chilling requirement for proper maturation of flowering buds, such as apples. Australia's cold season is not very long and specific apple varieties need strategic placement to obtain their required number of hours below 10°C.

Grow frost-susceptible plants slightly downhill from hard structures such as houses, sheds and tanks. They will be protected from the cold air as it flows around them and downhill. Long grass or densely planted rows of frost-tolerant plants slightly off contour also divert frost. Or, if there is nowhere to divert the frost to, let it bank up behind them. Ensure they have low limbs to stop the frost going under and plant downhill from them.

Be careful not to have massed barriers, such as a dense hedge, just below frost-susceptible plants. Such a structure can block cold air drainage, causing it to bank up and inflict damage. You could cut low holes out of it for drainage and to enhance community hide-and-seek.

A Frost Diversion Arc

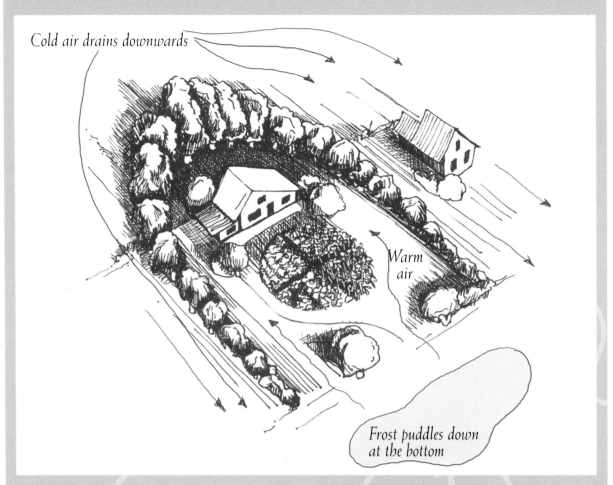

Cold air drains downwards

Warm air

Frost puddles down at the bottom

A Frost Diversion Arc deflects frost. It is on a hill, with the highest point at the top and the sides going around the plants that need protection. As cold air drains down the hill it flows either side of the arc. When it reaches the bottom of the hill it pushes warmer air up into the arc to those plants that need it most. If the slope is northerly facing the arc can double up as a sun trap. Sun traps increase and store heat in the soil, water and structures with a high thermal mass. This also helps prevent frost.

In places where you are unable to drain cold air away, such as on flat areas, first grow a 'nursery' crop — there are many short-lived, frost-tolerant plants, such as some acacias, that are perfect for this purpose. After a few years, when these are well established, young trees that are frost-susceptible can be planted among these 'nurse' trees, protecting them from frost until they're established. Ensure they get enough water and fertiliser as there will be competition. When the vulnerable species have grown up and are safe, cut out the nurse crop and use it for firewood or mulch.

Ponds and dams store heat and let out warmth at night and early morning, reducing the chance of frost.

In autumn and winter grow sprawling frost-tolerant plants over the mulch in the vegetable garden so the mulch doesn't loose heat so quickly and frost over.

Sometimes the shock of the sun hitting frozen plants in the morning damages their cells. Aim to shield vulnerable plants from early morning winter sun so they can thaw more gently. If possible, place the most susceptible plants on the western or southern side of a slope or house so they can thaw out before the morning sun strikes them.

Design overhead sprinklers in the most vital areas, such as the vegetable garden. To reduce frost damage jump out of bed on frosty mornings and turn them on before the sun hits. Position the pipes where they won't freeze.

Frost-tolerant Fruit Trees

It is difficult to define species that are frost tolerant as there are so many variables. For example, different varieties have different levels of frost tolerance or an unexpected late frost could come through and kill the buds on an early-flowering species. So this list is just a beginning. Talk to your local nursery and look around to see what is growing well in similar conditions, and in the micro-climates you can create.

To help with greater definition of frost tolerance I've marked those stalwarts that are capable of handling below -5°C with an 'S'. Those trees that can't handle such cold temperatures I've marked with a 'Y'. In most instances these can handle light frost as long as they are protected while young until they reach about 2–3 metres.

Apple – **S**	Hazelnut – **S**	Pecan – **S**
Apricot – **S**	Japanese raisin tree – **S**	Persimmon – **S**
Black mulberry – **S**	Kiwi fruit – **S**	Pistachio – **S**
Blueberry – **S**	Lemon – **Y**	Plum – **S**
Carambola – **Y**	Longan – **Y**	Pomegranate – **S**
Carob – **S**	Loquat – **S**	Pummelo – **Y**
Cherry – **S**	Macadamia – **Y**	Quince – **S**
Cumquat – **Y**	Mandarin – **Y**	Red cherry guava – **S**
Feijoa – **S**	Nectarine – **S**	Tamarillo – **Y**
Fig – **S**	Olive – **S**	Tangello – **Y**
Grapefruit – **Y**	Orange – **Y**	Walnut – **S**
Grumichama – **Y**	Peach – **S**	White sapote – **Y**
Guava – **Y**	Pear – **S**	Yellow cherry guava – **S**

Designing in Detail

This chapter presents three of my detailed designs:

The Bush Food Snack Track, Our Water Management

Plan and Our Vegetable Garden at Work. Then I'll let

you in on some of my blunders. Doctors bury their

mistakes (and call their place a practice); architects cover

theirs in ivy; mine are here for all to see. Fortunately

they're mitigated by some clever design moves...

*Designs interweave details like
the spirals of a sunflower.*

A Detailed Design is a more intricately planned section of the Concept Design (see page 92). Whereas the broad-brush Concept Design determines where things fit in the big picture, the Detailed Design determines how they will look. A Detailed Design is more precise and gets into the nitty gritty — more exact measurements, details on specific plants and how they'll size up, contours, how things will interact and affect each other. This precision can make the prospect of Detailed Designs a bit daunting to begin with. Yet the benefits become obvious soon and making the connections can be like playing a fun game of chess.

Drawing a Detailed Design

Select an area that you would like to plan in more detail. On a large piece of paper draw that part of the garden, including what already exists (see Drawing a Base Map on page 70). On top of this draw all planned infrastructure as well as the all-important pathways. Make a list of all the plant species and varieties you want. Work out their basic mature width and then make circular cut outs of them to scale. Dance them around on the map until you find places they seem to fit, maybe even benefiting the plants around them. The following three designs and examples of our mistakes may give you some more ideas. Also look at the next chapter on reducing pests and the following one on interesting plants for possible inclusions.

The caper white butterfly.

All the plants are placed in relation to each other.

The Bush Food Snack Track

I selected around 25 plants I wanted to go in the snack track and then planted them according to my following criteria:

- Aromatic plants to go along the path: the myrtles — lemon-scented, carol and aniseed.
- Stunning plants to be placed where they are easily seen: Davidson's plum, small-leaved lilly pilly.
- Tasty fast-food snacks to be accessible to children: native raspberries, midyim berries.
- Large trees placed where they will shade the pathways but not hog the sun from other plants.

Bushes that will eventually be surrounded by trees are selected for their ability to handle the transition from full sun to dappled shade: native lime, midyim berry.

- Genetically ancient trees (with stories from the dinosaur era) to be prominent: the bolwarra.
- Prickly trees to remind cheeky kids not to take a shortcut over the steep bank: finger lime, round lime.
- Plants that like good drainage to be on the dam wall: pigface, Warrigal greens.

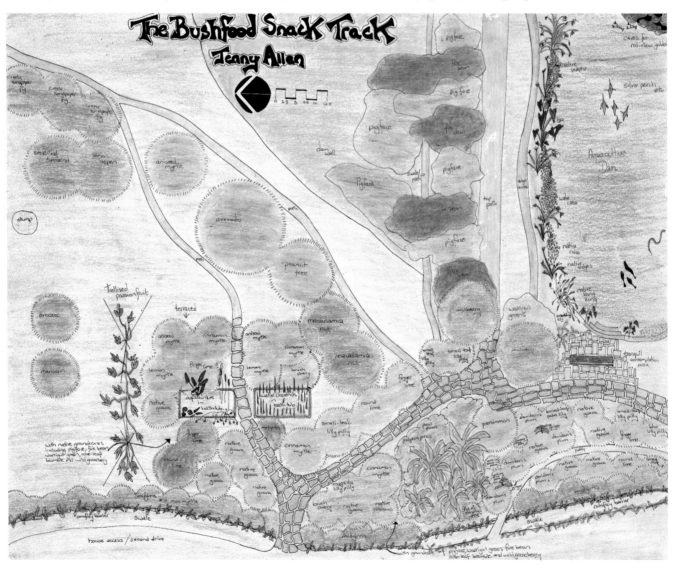

118

Our Water Management Plan

Water is such an important issue for us. Our Concept Design alone couldn't solve the main problems of it flowing under the house and making small rivers through the garden while simultaneously deserting the areas most in need. I set out to find as many inter-linked solutions in a thematic plan as possible. Every part of the garden is taken into account. We keep the water as high as possible for as long as possible and try not to let it escape — unless we have too much.

The design is intended to show us how to:

- Capture and direct water away from the house, mainly with a series of swales, slightly off contour, on the hill above. Any water that escapes these is caught in an agricultural pipe below the driveway and directed to bananas.
- Irrigate about 30 fruit trees with the water from the Biolytix Filter.
- Stop stormwater destructively converging by using terraces and swales to slow down the flow and spread the water.
- Send stormwater from the vegie garden to fruit trees that can handle it.
- Use a series of agricultural pipes to passively spread the tank overflow water to moisture-loving fruit trees.

Our Water Map

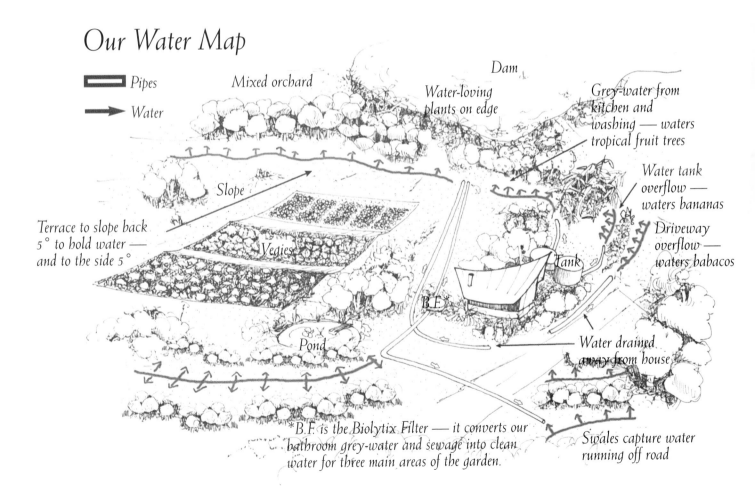

Pipes
Water

Mixed orchard

Dam
Water-loving plants on edge

Grey-water from kitchen and washing — waters tropical fruit trees

Slope

Water tank overflow — waters bananas

Terrace to slope back 5° to hold water — and to the side 5°

Driveway overflow — waters babacos

Vegies

Tank

B.F.*

Pond

Water drained away from house

*B.F. is the Biolytix Filter — it converts our bathroom grey-water and sewage into clean water for three main areas of the garden.

Swales capture water running off road

Our Vegetable Garden at Work

A vegetable garden can be attractive as well as productive. Using the 10 Design Principles (see page 32) it is possible to have nature do a large proportion of the work.

1. Multiple Uses — The plants growing up the garden arch maximise vertical space while shading heat-susceptible plants such as lettuce and coriander.

2. Zoning — The plants we use the most, such as herbs, are closest to the house.

3. Smart Placement — Cold winter air flowing towards the vegie garden is re-directed down the road by the tall trees. In summer these same trees block out the hot afternoon sun. Just a bit further round to the north-west the trees are smaller so the winter afternoon sun can shine through.

4. Elevational Planning — Plants that like good drainage grow on the higher side of the terrace or on the slopes between the terraces.

5. Recycling Resources — The comfrey border at the base of the garden captures and stores run-off nutrients and we cut it back, using it as fertiliser and mulch.

6. Growing Up — We grow many perennial vegies as they are more productive and less work over the long term, such as asparagus which produces for up to 20 years.

7. Diversity — We have up to 10 different types of greens.

8. Homemade Insurance — If we're away and there's a hot spell, our insurance policy automatically kicks in. The vegies are protected in many different ways. They are: often deep-rooted perennials or, if not, they may be heat tolerant; shaded from hot afternoon summer sun; planted under the arch; planted in different niches on the terrace according to their water needs; and/or mulched to keep moisture in.

9. Using Nature's Gifts — Nitrogen-fixing bushes, such as crotalaria, are on the edge of the garden. We cut back their soft branches and use them as mulch.

10. See Solutions, Not Problems — We turned the initial problem of a steep and dry slope into terraces which we can access easily. The terraces also make it easy for us to plant out the vegies according to their different moisture requirements.

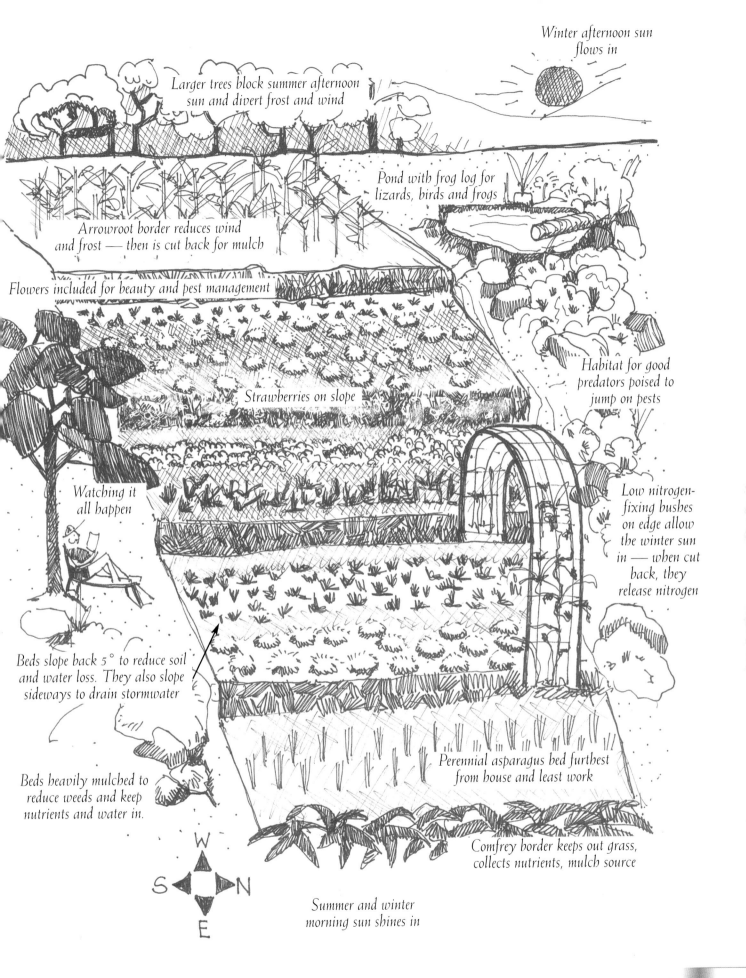

Winter afternoon sun flows in

Larger trees block summer afternoon sun and divert frost and wind

Pond with frog log for lizards, birds and frogs

Arrowroot border reduces wind and frost — then is cut back for mulch

Flowers included for beauty and pest management

Strawberries on slope

Habitat for good predators poised to jump on pests

Watching it all happen

Low nitrogen-fixing bushes on edge allow the winter sun in — when cut back, they release nitrogen

Beds slope back 5° to reduce soil and water loss. They also slope sideways to drain stormwater

Perennial asparagus bed furthest from house and least work

Beds heavily mulched to reduce weeds and keep nutrients and water in.

Comfrey border keeps out grass, collects nutrients, mulch source

W
S — N
E

Summer and winter morning sun shines in

With Hindsight

Although I planned in detail, some things inevitably went awry. Here are four examples of awkward features of the garden that haven't yet been resolved.

You can't solve a problem using the same kind of thinking that got you into the problem in the first place. Albert Einstein

Grapes are fine in Zone 1, as we pick them daily when they ripen to beat the birds. The hardy bush foods just behind them would be better placed in Zone 4 but I don't have the heart to cut them out now as they're thriving in this prime spot. A valuable learning experience that will probably end with chainsaws.

Bush Foods Too Close

When I was starting to plan our garden, bush foods were one of my main focuses. Consequently, the Bush Food Snack Track was located in a prime position: relatively close to the house. Here the plants are protected from wind and frost, fed by the composting system, and outside my office window so I could watch their every move. Naturally the bush food trees thrived, yet they are so hardy they don't really need the luxury of such a pampered micro-climate.

Since then, our interest in new tastes has led to a fascination with exotic fruit trees. Now we want to extend our range of these to include highly sensitive trees that demand the protected warm micro-climates to be found around the house and the dam. Where the bush foods are happily growing would be ideal.

I learnt two big lessons from this: that Zoning is vital, and to be careful enthusiasm doesn't override it. The bush foods were always going to grow tall and need little maintenance; however, I was so enthralled by them that I planned for them to stay under my wing. Now they've outgrown me — yet they're stuck in the nest.

Comfrey Comes Free but Charges Later

For some, comfrey is the wonder plant. For others…the blunder plant. On a positive note it blocks creeping grass and weeds; makes a great mulch source; helps activate the compost and liquid fertiliser; and is also called knit-bone as it supposedly helps heal fractures. For dinner parties I sometimes deep-fry the young leaves in batter — they surprise the guests with their fish-like taste and shock them with their innocent green. With all these benefits, I initially embraced comfrey. And comfrey embraced me. I not only planted it along perimeters but interspersed it through the vegie garden. Later I thought it took up too much prime location space and attempted to restrict its growth.

It was hard work. Its octopus-like roots spread through the garden and meant we had to scramble around pulling them out, even the small tips, so they wouldn't multiply. After the last dig, we

Native bees love the comfreys' spiral inflorescences.

covered any regrowth with double cardboard and mulch. Fortunately, after 10 months of digging and smothering, the comfrey is now becoming weak and spindly and we are finally on top of it.

One way to stop comfrey marching like a Triffid army is to plant it on the garden edge with perennials, such as pepino and asparagus, next to them on the vegie-garden side. This helps to avoid accidentally cutting off any of the comfrey's roots while digging, which causes them to throw up new plants and spread further.

A comfrey border needs to be in the right place if it is to be a helpful friend, not a deep-rooted foe.

It would take a truckload of mulch to suppress a comfrey. I left this hay bale on top of a plant and within a month it had grown through it and out the top.

Fried Fish Eggs

I designed a daytime seating area to double as a fire-circle and deliver fast-food snacks. Enticed by the thought of afternoon dappled shade, we planted a Panama berry on the western side. In only two years we were delighting in its strawberry-flavoured fruit. (In Vietnam they are called fish eggs as, when bitten, they ooze tiny seeds in white jelly.) The fast-growing tree performs its job beautifully — exhibiting its umbrella shape. Unfortunately, when we have an open fire for barbecues, some of its leaves and small branches burn — I hear its silent screaming each time it happens. I realise now that it's not in the best place for its long-term comfort.

Our waterside snack bar — tamarillos just outside the bathroom window.

A tasty caramel-flavoured snack — the Panama berry.

Holy Smoke

Some plants cause discomfort. With the best of intentions, I planted three perennial tamarillo (tree tomato) bushes along the driveway. They play many roles here, hiding the gas bottles and welcoming us home with a handsome display of red and yellow egg-shaped fruit. We harvest the decorative fruit three months a year. In my eagerness to give them many uses I forgot one thing: they are formidable members of the tobacco family. Because they are next to the driveway, we brush past them, inadvertently absorbing the aroma of a stale ashtray. Every six months the poor gas-man has to forage amongst them to change our bottle. I've often wondered if, after returning to the truck, his boss tells him off for dangerously smoking on the job.

Clever Design Moves

I know when a part of our garden is successfully designed (and nature and I are working together), because it flourishes beyond expectation. Here is a pot-pourri of pleasing happenings in our garden, special gifts that money could rarely buy.

Of all the wonders in nature, a tree in summer is perhaps the most remarkable; with the possible exception of a moose singing 'Embraceable You' in spats. Woody Allen

A Shady Affair

People are less inclined to walk from their house to a shady spot in the garden if they have to walk through harsh sun to get there.

On a summer's day the tranquillity of shade is alluring. So we have a handsome umbrella-shaped shade tree beside the entrance to the verandah, with a camphor laurel seat beneath it. The tree reinforces the love affair between the house and garden. During the hot summer months, it's a perfect place to relax under its cooling shade. It's deciduous, so during the winter months when its leaves drop, the warming sun can stream into the house.

Visitors, both expected and unexpected, take to the spot enthusiastically. If we're running late, guests often wait here; the strawberries and raspberries help to keep them patient. If I'm not comfortable asking someone inside — a door-to-door salesperson I don't know, for instance — it's a handy place to sit and talk.

Extend the verandah without council approval — plant an umbrella-shaped tree.

The Cosmos in Our Vegie Garden

Pinks, oranges, reds and whites wave to the wind in the vegie garden. We planted an array of cosmos, not only to be charmed, but also because they have small flower parts. These small florets, like many members of the daisy family, offer readily accessible rich nectar to insects with tiny mouthpieces: for example, beneficial predators, like the hoverfly that eats garden pests, and parasitoids like the mini wasps that lay their eggs actually inside or on pests such as the cabbage white butterfly and aphids. Then when the parasitoids' eggs hatch into voracious larvae they are already inside or on top of their first warm meal. The seemingly serene is really a gory battlefield. Many other beautiful flowers such as Queen Anne's lace and sweet Alice also have small florets and attract predators and parasitoids. The chapter Test the Pests gives a lot more detail.

Zinnia, like cosmos, belongs to the daisy family. Like many members of this family, it produces easily accessible protein-rich pollen.

Cosmos, a cosmic lure for beneficial predators.

That Dam Edge

Water from several hectares of neighbours' land runs into our dam; with it, sadly, also come pollutants such as excess fertiliser and septic overflow. As a result the water and adjoining soil carry so many nutrients that the dam's edge is a prime site for a weed factory. Yet, by carefully designing the edge from the outset, beneficial plants have thrived here instead.

When the excavator made the dam we arranged for him to carve a one-metre ledge at the water's edge. Now native water-cleansing plants, such as sedges and juncas, flourish in this shallow water and help filter the surplus nutrients. Stunning cocoyams, with table-size elephant-ear leaves, also enjoy the constant moisture on the edge — although not as much as the sedges, so the cocoyams are planted slightly higher.

Further back we planted umbrella-shaped trees so that birds, such as the brilliant azure kingfisher, can dive from the lateral branches into the dam — though hopefully not to eat all our firetail gudgeons and young native silver and golden perch.

A dam ecosystem. A dam wall provides a range of habitats: sedges, being the natural transition from water to land plants, thrive in the capillary zone above the water line; moisture-loving cocoyams (and kids) rampage where it is slightly drier (see photo above); and on the well-drained crest, shallow-rooted citrus flourish.

The Living Trellis

We had two short-lived 8-metre high acacias that were due to come out in a couple of years. So we planted passionfruit vines under them. We slightly ring-barked the acacias so their foliage dropped gradually, enabling the sun to reach the passionfruit vine leaves as they ascended through the tree. Before long, the vine created a canopy — and the acacia looked like a strange tree with passionfruit leaves.

To support their leafy habit, passionfruits need a lot of nitrogen. Acacias are nitrogen-fixing trees — they take nitrogen from the air and, in conjunction with bacteria in the soil, they retain it in nodules along their roots and free it as a slow-release fertiliser, characteristically when the tree is stressed, pruned-back or dying. So, as the acacias slowly died, they fed the passionfruit. As a bonus, their branches became quite brittle, making it difficult for possums to climb to their outer edges for a feed of our potential breakfast. The crop remains mostly ours.

We ring-barked the slow-release, nitrogen-fertilising wattle and planted bliss bombs under it — Panama Gold passionfruit.

Each afternoon we forage under the trees and have a picnic — daily they drop about six big juicy yellow globes. Over three months that's over 500 sweet passionfruits we've been enjoying.

Nature has such bounty to offer, often for free, like this once-living trellis. So it is up to the gardener to plan ahead and reap the harvest. If we harmonise with our garden — replicating acacias' natural regeneration by replanting acacias every few years — it will develop in tune with us.

Our home-grown yellow passionfruits are the tastiest and juiciest in the neighbourhood — size does matter!

Moonlight Magic

Lining the pathway to my office are plants with white flowers, such as the native cat's whiskers. They reflect moonlight, guiding the way at night.

The only cat's whiskers we want in our garden are the native white ones. A single plant will provide enough cuttings to illuminate a moon-lit path.

Test
the Pests

Stop paying for pests to enjoy a luxury holiday, all meals

included. Design your garden to attract beneficial

predators and parasitoids — the so-called 'bennies' that

eat pests. The healthy balance of a garden depends on

the bennies' guerilla tactics, giving pests little chance to

bring along the sauce bottle and gorge themselves. Turn

them into paranoid wrecks before you become one yourself.

As an adult the dobson fly doesn't
eat much but its larvae are aquatic
and they eat a lot of mosquito
larvae and other potential pests.

Everyone seems to have at least one eccentric aunt. Mine is an obsessive gardener who heroically opens her property to the public, including an Edna Walling section, for Open Weekends. Once when she was in hospital she called me up. 'Come quickly,' she said. Upon my arrival, she pointed desperately at a tired bunch of flowers that the nurse was about to throw out. I didn't see much cause for concern. Then she showed me the two ladybirds on the flowers. She picked them off, put them in a paper bag and requested I put them on the rose bushes in her garden. They were to help keep her aphids under control. I walked down the hospital corridor, my bag of ladybirds clutched in hand, relieved that that was the only problem.

A ladybird eats up to 1100 aphids before she produces her first eggs.

Among the scholarly lingo of the integrated pest management specialists is the word 'bennies'. Bennies is the name they give to pest predators and parasitoids because both are beneficial to the garden.

My aunt knows her pests. She is expertly equipped to deal with them, wherever she is, whatever condition she may be in.

Some people attack their gardens, dressed in commando outfits, poised to spray toxic chemicals over anything that moves, be it pest or pest predator. Yet, by swapping their spray gun for inquisitive eyes — even a magnifying glass or hand lens — they might discover a teeming microcosm of predators interacting with their pests.

Pests, like humans, seem to have the idea that nature is theirs to exploit. Many people are conditioned to respond to this audacity with chemicals. However, no matter how much they spray the problem is often not only left unsolved,

One of the thousands of frogs we accommodate to eat our mosquitoes, flies and other pests takes time out for a spa.

it can get worse or more complicated. This is because pests are often a symptom of a system out of whack, not a cause.

In the 1880s, the Californian citrus industry was devastated by an insect called cottony

cushion scale. Controls the industry relied on for the previous 30 years, such as cyanide gas, failed. Then they imported 524 Vedalia ladybirds from Australia. Within a few weeks the ladybirds had virtually wiped out the scale and within a year there was little of it left in the state. The ladybird is such a success story it has been packaged and sent to over 500 countries, where it's still doing a great job. Interestingly it is where there is heavy pesticide use — for unrelated problems — that it is not so effective. The ladybirds are annihilated in the process.

There's much to be learned from this remarkable story. It shows the power of using

The beauty of an iris will transfigure into…the beauty of a butterfly. Unless your life depends upon it, let caterpillars do their thing. Few enough will make it to adulthood and they will be a reliable food source for predators.

pest predators for long-term pest management — a far better ploy than using pesticides, whether chemical or organic.

If there were no predators, we'd be in a lot of trouble. The authors of *Common Sense Pest Control* give the example of the rampant common housefly. Apparently it can lay 600 eggs at a time. In hot weather these are ready to mate in about six days. With this rate of reproduction, in one summer a pair of flies could lead to so many generations of offspring that they would create a black buzzing blanket thousands of feet thick around the planet. (Maybe they could fill up the gaping big hole in the ozone layer.)

Predators and natural checks and balances would prevent this happening. According to one of the world's finest authorities on spiders and the author of *The World Of Spiders*, Dr W. S. Bristowe, spiders in Britain would eat 270,000 tonnes of insects in an average year — that's about the weight of everyone in Sydney and Melbourne after Christmas lunch. Few creatures work as hard and as adeptly as spiders, doing a job we're not good at, nor enjoy.

Pesticides can instantly destroy spiders and other predators. Most conventional pest control ignores the delicate ecological balance.

The story of the two-spotted mite highlights this. Before pesticides were used widely it was rarely known, yet now it has become a pest. This could be because one of its main predators, the predatory mite, has been sprayed by mistake while other pests — probably ones it was eating — were being targeted.

The spraying of pesticides could well have obliterated many predators — we may never know. At this stage less than 10% of Australian insects are classified. Let's not create more pests with pesticide. Emulating natural ploys in the garden helps nature manage herself.

We really wanted to see what these bizarre caterpillars turned into.…but so far they have all been predated. So much for our over-protective concern that there were too many of them on the custard apple tree!

Parasitoids

Parasitoids are the unsung heroes of a balanced garden ecology. While predators, such as ground beetles, just rush in and eat a single pest in a meal, parasitoids do it more slowly, but their impact is massive. As many are small and they are not as flirtatious as predators, such as dragonflies, they are often overlooked.

Parasitoids come from five insect orders and are mainly wasps, including mini-wasps and flies. Most of the adults feed on nectar, pollen and/or sap while their larvae eat out the insides of pests.

In the top picture the ichneumon wasp is inserting its hypodermic ovipositor into a caterpillar, trying to inject its eggs into it. When these hatch, the maggot-like larvae will eat the non-vital insides of their living host. As you can imagine, the caterpillar goes through a lot of pain in this drawn-out process.

In the bottom photo a cabbage white caterpillar is in its final stages of life as the fattened larvae tunnel their way out of its body to form yellow silk cocoons. One of them has already hatched into a wasp — which is on top of the caterpillar body. This wasp will soon start the gory procedure all over again with another fresh caterpillar.

It is often children who discover this process. They capture a caterpillar in a jar so they can watch it transform into a butterfly. Yet when they look at it a few days later they are in for a birds and bees surprise – a gang of wasps has emerged instead.

It's important to be able to recognise the different stages of bennies and where they live and feed. This ensures, for example, that you don't annihilate the prickly looking ladybird larvae, or their habitat, and then wonder why there are so few ladybirds around. Both the larvae and adults are voracious killers of pests and are on your side.

The highly efficient circus team is keen to move in to your place and sort out your pests for free. In fact many of them are already there.

Garden ecology is about who's eating who. A little bit of knowledge saves a lot of time and effort. To accomplish more with less work, learn about your main pests and evaluate if they are so deleterious that they could kill some plants. Identify which predators move in to dine on the pests. It's tempting to think that if something is ugly, it must be detrimental to the garden but in the garden often the opposite is true: the predacious lacewing larva looks like a miniature crocodile with jaws to match. It sucks out the entrails of its prey, such as aphids, and then has the gall to stack their withered shells on its back as camouflage. A wolf in sheep's clothing.

It is often just before the pests are really harmful that the predator population takes off and cleans them up. The beneficial predators have been doing their work experience for thousands of years, many for millions. So it's worth introducing yourself to them and have them working on your side. The predators will be able to manage your biosmart, interactive Eden even while you're sleeping in, on holiday or in a hospital bed.

Now on to meet the bennies.

The holes in this arrowroot leaf were made by a caterpillar. Predatory wasps search for caterpillars around holes like these. In the hope of prey, the predatory wasps also hang around our naturally holey monsteria leaves (see photo on page 209). Maybe the monsteria's holes have evolved through natural selection to encourage wasps to protect them?

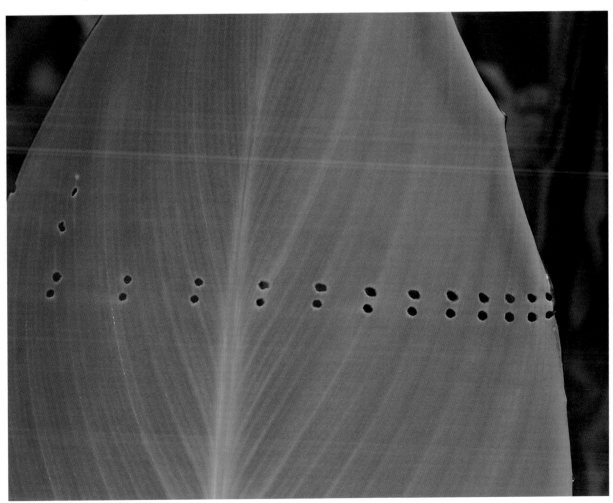

Beneficial Pest Predators and Parasitoids

All these photos were taken in a 40-metre radius of our house, highlighting the astounding range of bennies quietly at work.

Assassin Bugs

These vicious-looking creatures pierce pests with their large proboscis, paralysing and killing them. They simply inject a powerful enzyme into their prey, liquefying its internal organs so they can drink them. The potential broth on their menu includes caterpillars, grasshoppers, green vegetable bugs and the harlequin and crusader bugs.

The ornate assassin bug nymph stabs its dagger-like proboscis into its prey then drinks them like a smoothie.

Bats *(small, insectivorous ones)*

At night they dart around catching up to 600 insects an hour, according to Linda Woodrow's *The Permaculture Home Garden*.

Beetles

These are some of the most effective and numerous predators. With their fearsome jaws, many rip apart caterpillars, nematodes, march flies, thrips, cutworms, larval fruit fly, slugs, snails, aphids, scale, ants and termites, as well as grasshopper and snails' eggs. Anything that eats a fruit fly or its larvae is something I want to encourage. They often feed at night and can be quite colourful, shining iridescent black, bronze or green. They prey in both the larval and adult stages and many live in the ground, as well as burrowing under surface debris. Rove beetles are particularly beneficial. See also ladybirds.

A predatory aphid-eating beetle.

Birds *(including robins, wrens, drongos, willie wagtails, silver-eyes, fantails, honeyeaters and flycatchers)*

Everyone knows that birds eat a wide range of pests, but there is one species we are especially delighted with. The drongos are keeping our seemingly unpalatable bronze orange citrus bug under control. It beats squishing the bugs with rubber gloves while they squirt pungent liquid at us. Out of respect we would like to officially change the drongo's name to one that holds more dignity. We are also erecting podiums for these winners to stand on — stakes near our citrus trees. The drongos perch on these to get strategic surveillance advantage.

Centipedes

Probably not a family favourite, given their potentially nasty sting, centipedes are nonetheless a handy gardening ally. One of their favourite meals is slugs. (Sadly centipedes are also partial to worms.)

Dragonflies/Damselflies

The adults are aerial gymnasts, using their wonderful wrap-around compound eyes to quickly snatch mosquitoes, flies and other small flying insects. At any time on a warm day there will be at least ten in our garden catching insects. As an airline company will tell you, it takes a lot of fuel to keep an object airborne;

A damsel in distress — damselflies are so voracious that they sometimes eat their own kind.

fortunately for us dragonflies and damselflies have perfected mid-flight refuelling. Their larvae live in water and devour hundreds of mosquito wrigglers, a double bonus.

At rest dragonflies hold their wings out, damselflies keep them together.

Frogs

Frogs eat a wide range of insects. Encourage them by building a pond and installing a frog log so they can get in and out easily. Provide lots of plants and other hiding spots for protection.

The frog is an ever-vigilant guardian of our young mangoes.

Hoverflies

In order to avoid being attacked, adult hoverflies mimic bees and wasps. However, they are easy to identify as they hover around plants before darting on prey, such as aphids, beetles and caterpillars. They eat nectar and pollen, especially from open-type flowers. They lay their eggs amongst aphids so their offspring can hatch to a gastronomic delight.

In contrast to their zooming parents, the larvae look sluggish and just hang around the aphids — piercing and sucking their innards. They suffer badly if pesticides are sprayed.

Lacewings

From the moment the voracious lacewing larvae hatch they use their formidable jaws to pierce and suck out the innards of prey such as thrip eggs, white fly, aphids, mealybugs, scale and mites. Then the miniature crocodiles transform into luminous green, fairy-like adults, mainly feeding on pollen and honeydew. Watch out for them flitting and flirting around nightlights.

There are two main types of lacewing: the green and the brown. The brown lacewing's eggs can be found attached to leaves. The green lacewing lays its eggs on the end of a silk stalk so it is out of the way of many predators. However, their predators include cannibalistic brothers and sisters who have just hatched. It pays to be the oldest in the lacewing family. The lacewing larvae are so effective in helping manage aphids that they are produced commercially and released in greenhouses and onto agricultural crops.

Three life stages of a green lacewing. Watching a lacewing larva in action makes you glad it's only a few millimetres long.

Ladybirds

These charming insects come in an assortment of colours and spots. Both the larvae and adults devour aphids, mealy bugs, mites, whitefly, psyllids and scale insects. (Although don't be duped by the 26- and 28-spotted ladybirds, which have jumped on the goodwill bandwagon — they eat plants). Out of all the predators the ladybirds play one of the most important roles in keeping aphids under control. In the larval stage they can eat 200–600 aphids and then the adults eat 200–500 before producing their first eggs. If you watch carefully you may see an aphid successfully kick away a small ladybird larva that is trying to

This lifecycle shows how the ladybird gets her spots. Both nymphs and adults are efficient predators of aphids.

attack it. Ladybirds are much bigger than aphids, yet an aphid may still escape by 'waxing' — secreting a drop of oily liquid which solidifies on the ladybird's mouthparts, putting it out of action for around half an hour while it cleans up. However, if the ladybird wins out it only takes it a minute or so for it to devour an aphid and then move onto the next one. We saw one species sit down to a dozen fresh caterpillar eggs.

Unfortunately the ladybirds often don't clean up a colony of pests. If you watch carefully they like to skim over the surface and go for the easier pickings.

There are over 4000 species of ladybirds worldwide and over 250 in Australia alone.

Lizards

Lizards eat a wide range of pests such as cockroaches, moths, snails, grasshoppers and beetles. For protection from birds and cats, they live under rocks, logs and leaf litter.

Cockroaches are reputed to be able to survive a nuclear holocaust but few young ones survive a hungry skink or gecko.

Long-legged Flies

There are 320 species in Australia and many of the adults and larvae are predators, killing soft-bodied pests such as aphids and various larvae. Their larvae live in leaf litter and the soil. This is also where the fruit fly larvae live and I wonder if they eat them as well.

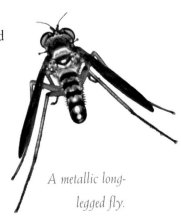

A metallic long-legged fly.

Praying Mantises

Both the larvae and adults eat a range of small pests, including the cabbage riddler moth. Often they can be seen hanging around colonies of pests — not necessarily to eat the pests but sometimes to eat the pests' predators when they dart in for the kill. All the same, their presence is a good indicator of a balanced ecosystem.

To sneak up on prey and to protect themselves many change their colour according to the surroundings. They are quite characteristic — holding their forelegs as if they're praying.

Mantises are just as likely to eat a bennie as a pest. This one lies in wait for hoverflies that drink the nectar of the parsley flower.

Robber Flies

These are medium to large flies that catch pests on the wing. They also inject their prey with an enzyme so they can drink them.

The robber fly — don't be put off by its name and hairy beard — this Ned Kelly is part of your gang.

Snakes

We respect our snakes and in return they help keep mice and rat populations down; so there is less damage to the corn and pumpkin. Most snakes die if they eat a cane toad, which indirectly leads to more mice and rats being around, so we kill our cane toads. Fortunately the harmless keelback snakes are able to eat young toads and survive.

Snakes are not naturally vicious and would prefer to leave humans alone. It is when they're disturbed or provoked that they're more likely to attack. So we have wide paths, with a surface that is easy to see them on. When we are outside at night we illuminate the paths. We watch out for them, not only on warm days and nights, but in really wet times as well. They can be extra vicious if they've been flooded out of their home, as my father painfully discovered.

He was helping round up cattle onto dry land in the Queensland floods of 1991. After a hard day's work he was washing his feet at the front of the homestead and trod on a distressed and highly poisonous eastern brown snake (*Pseudonaja textilis*). It bit him three times and he was rushed to hospital. The doctor had only ever administered two doses of anti-venom at any one time, yet he gave Dad ten doses. This alone made him sick and blacken.

The opalescent gleam of a dwarf crown snake.

Spiders

These highly evolved creatures are probably the most important of all predators but unfortunately our world is so human centred that they also have a bad name. If it wasn't for spiders we might not even be here at all — it could be a world run by insects. They also eat some predators. They live in webs, plants, houses, logs and leaf litter and are very susceptible to sprays.

Maybe the two-spined spider mimics a tree snake's face to frighten other predators.

Wasps (including mini-wasps)

Wasps may be predators or parasitoids, or both. They are nearly all useful, attacking most pests, ranging from nymphs of small aphids and white fly to caterpillars, sawflies, lawn and wood-boring beetles, grasshoppers and cockroaches. Some wasps' larvae, such as those from the ichneumon family and the tiny *Apanteles* species, live either on or in the bodies of their host, such as the cabbage butterfly larvae and sawfly larvae. They eat the hosts insides in preparation for becoming an adult. Many adult wasps have small mouthparts and so feed on open flowers.

The two main superfamilies of parasitic wasps are the Ichneumonoidae and Chalcidoidae (of which there are 100,000 species, many not named). According to Henry and Marjorie Townes, who probably have the largest collection of wasps in existence, 'The Ichneumonoidae is one of the largest of all animal groups; it includes more species than the entire Vertebrata and more than any other family, with the possible exception of the Curculionidae [weevils]'.

If you think aphids are too small for parasitoid wasps such as these to bother with, consider that some dust-sized wasps (0.15 millimetres long) parasitise even tinier insect eggs.

Attracting Bennies

*A*ttracting bennies to your garden is usually a matter of emulating the complexity of nature, rather than paring it down to the bare minimum. Provide them with some form of protection from their own predators. Densely planted perennial shrubs around the garden protect insect predators, such as small birds, from bigger, bolshier birds and sneaky cats. It helps if the bushes are grouped in blocks, rather than long and thin, so there is less edge for intruders, such as cats, to exploit. If the bushes are prickly they will protect the birds even better. In this niche-with-a view apartment in the new housing estate, they can sit safely, poised to pounce on pests.

Bennies often need protein and sugar in the form of pollen and nectar. But many have short mouthparts and they often find it difficult to access rich nectar in deep-throated flowers. Instead they feed from flowers with tiny florets, especially from the carrot and daisy families. The carrot family has flowers with many clustered florets. They supply plentiful food, but only for short periods as they don't flower for long. On the other hand, the daisy family has less nectar but flowers for longer.

In *Your Edible Landscape Naturally* R. Kourik likens the combination of carrot and daisy families to an

Beneficial hoverflies don't have drinking straws attached — so serve their champagne nectar in tiny umbel cups. These ones are provided by the coriander flower.

Plants That May Attract Pest Predators

The following list has been compiled from a number of sources including *Your Edible Landscape Naturally*, the Green Harvest Mail Order Catalogue and our own observation. The attractiveness of the plants to predators will differ between areas — it pays to do your own research. Green Harvest Organic Suppliers sells a lot of these insect-attracting plants as well as a 'Good Bug Mix' that contains a mixture of many of the seeds. The Mix can be sown throughout the garden, although it is best to keep it out of the vegie patch.

Carrot Family — umbrella-shaped flowers

Caraway

Carrot

Celery

Coriander

Dill

Parsley

Queen Anne's lace

The Sunflower Family — tiny florets clustered together

Cosmos

Marigold

Tansy

Yarrow

Pea and Bean Family with extra nectaries

Clover: white and red

Lucerne/alfalfa

Lupin

Woolly pod vetch

Broccoli Family

Broccoli

Mustard

Radish, including daikon

Sweet Alice (white alyssum)

Some other plants — you may want to add to this list as you observe more

Blue eyes

Buckwheat

Rue

orchestra of food — the daisy family provides continuous melody and nectar and the carrot family comes in with exciting drumming performances and short feasts throughout the year.

Other plants in flower also provide accessible nectar, such as those from broccoli and the pea family, the latter having extra floral nectaries. So, when possible, allow them to flower profusely and try to lengthen their flowering period with judicious pruning.

Easily accessible water during dry periods is also a lure. This may be derived from the sprinkler, dew, a pond or dam. If there is no water around they may look for it elsewhere — and never return. If you meet all the bennies' needs they will thank you many times over with pest-free fruit on the table.

Integrated Pest Management

This is a scientific term many permaculturalists have adapted to suit their philosophy of gardening organically and sustainably. IPM, as it is often called, is a multi-pronged, holistic approach to managing pests. It incorporates a number of different, but complementary, strategies. One of the underlying themes of all the strategies is habitat management in conjunction with attracting a diverse range of plants, insects, birds, reptiles, amphibians and other creatures. As a consequence of this more balanced ecology, there is less need for chemical intervention.

Attracting bennies is an important IPM strategy. Ten other ploys for controlling pests are described below. An integrated pest manager tries to use as many of these as possible at any one time.

IPM recognises that pests can only ever be managed, not eliminated. Controlling pests with chemicals wipes out many important members of the food chain in specific areas, including both pests and predators. This puts the ecology out of balance and when nature's out of whack, one of the first things to come back unchecked and in force are multitudes of pests.

Effective Pest Control Ploys

Common sense is a great weapon against pests.

1 Grow plants that don't satisfy the pest's palate but still satisfy yours. Strongly aromatic plants, such as the curry tree , are too pungent for pests to attack, yet are pungent-perfect to flavour meals. Cocoyams and plants that are high in oxalates, such as Warrigal greens, need to be cooked to be palatable — if you don't like them uncooked, chances are pests won't either.

2 If certain fruit and vegetables are known to be susceptible to pest attack when ripening, design for them to be in visible areas that you visit a lot so they can be harvested as they ripen and before pesky possums pinch them. This is particularly important for fruit such as babacos and figs.

3 If pests are eating a particular plant, then try to substitute it with something that gives you a similar flavour but is less pest susceptible. For example, strawberries may be substituted with acerola cherries; they have a strawberry flavour but are not as susceptible to attack.

4 Plant more than you need, so losing some isn't so upsetting.

5 Healthy soil produces healthy plants. Just as poor nutrition makes humans vulnerable to viruses and bacteria, so plants depend on a balanced diet. Fertile soil helps them build strong cell walls that are more difficult for pests to penetrate. And if the plants are nibbled or attacked by viruses—which are often spread by pests—they stand a better chance of bouncing back. It also helps to have a diversity of soil life. This leads to a diversity of pest predators. If necessary, improve the soil before planting and keep

plants well fed, well mulched and weed- and grass-free.

6 Place plants where their needs are met naturally and they are rarely stressed. Ensure they will have enough sun, wind protection, drainage and space; if not, put strategies in place that ensure they have the best chance.

7 Don't be seduced into growing a juicy delicate peach if it is known to be a pest magnet in your area.

8 Research the plant species that are the most pest resilient, and which variety of that species is the hardiest. Some of these varieties may fall short in another area, such as succulence, so try hedging your bets and plant a variety known for juiciness and one known for its pest resistance. For example, grow the luscious but risky Grosse Lisse tomatoes, as well as their hardier wild cousin — the cherry tomatoes.

9 Gather good-quality varieties displaying hardy, pest-resistant genes. And grow species that quickly jump back from pest attack without needing assistance, like taro. Ours had its lush leaves decimated by caterpillars, as is common to our region. Within three weeks it jumped back, with every new leaf intact.

10 Offer distractions and botanical riddles that put you ahead of the pests. For

Pests often detect what they are going to eat by its aroma. So help conceal vunerable plants with different odours and shapes, like those of the spring onion.

example, hide the silhouette and aroma of vulnerable plants by inter-planting them with other plants, including strongly aromatic ones: members of the onion family can help to conceal tasty vegies. Also plant any one species over a wide area (provided they don't need to cross-pollinate) so even if pests attack one, the others remain safely hidden away.

Exciting and Unusual Edible Plants

The ever-inventive tendency of nature is being whittled down by the homogenisation of many nurseries and gardens. Diversity, not uniformity, is the very essence of nature and, by association, of permaculture. A well-selected variety of plants ensures your garden will suffer less from pests and be more stable, producing a constant stream of food and fascination.

Aborigines in parts of northern Australia relish the pink lotus.

Pepino.

Punctuate an apple pie or smoothie with zingy small-leaved lilly pillies.

Many modern nurseries cater to the lowest common denominator in search of the highest profit. Often, as a result of mass-marketing, people struggle to sustain hard-to-grow plants when more appropriate and tasty varieties can be readily substituted and cultivated. In this chapter we look at a range of exciting and hardy fruit trees, herbs, vegetables, and bush foods that prosper in a wide variety of climatic zones. They awaken the senses with fresh flavours, smells, textures, stories and other surprises.

There is merit in variety itself. It provides more points of contact with life and leads away from uniformity and monotony.
Liberty Hyde Bailey

Inspiration can spring from many places. Take an experimental edible journey around markets, quality supermarkets and specialty fruit shops —especially Asian and Mediterranean. Try new flavours.

Other places worth visiting are specialist nurseries, botanic gardens and private gardens open to the public.

You could then list any unusual edible plants you would like to grow and draw them onto your Detailed Design.

Fruit Trees

Babaco
Carica pentagona

This mysterious hybrid pawpaw is from the mountains, originally the Andes. It looks like a yellow, five-sided rocket: soon to take off in Australia.

Unveiled to the world in 1922, New Zealand recently tried to grasp its potential. In an attempt to emulate their kiwi fruit success they promoted it vigorously. But this time the world wasn't conned into believing it was the Kiwis' fruit. In fact, most people noticed very little. Humankind was either too busy or saturated with globe-trotting fruit hype for subtle tastes.

I urge the home gardener to find time to appreciate the babaco. It's a hardy producer with a delicate flavour. The 40-centimetre fruit tastes of sherbet, melon and diluted pineapple, laced with a tinge of strawberry or even rose. It has a long shelf life, keeping for about two weeks at room temperature and in the fridge for about a month. Its versatile, fluffy flesh and soft skin can titillate fruit salads or be blended with fruit drinks such as orange juice to make a light thirst-quencher.

The attractive 2-metre plant's yields are reliable. Each of our six bushes produce about 15 large fruits annually — and there are reports of up to 100. Fortunately, it has high mountains coded into its DNA so it doesn't need to be genetically spliced with a polar bear to survive the cold. It can tolerate -2°C — conditions that

The delicate petals of the babaco flower unzip to reveal a perfectly formed fruit.

The babaco's tasty fruit juice starts to flow when the oranges are finishing.

would numb the common pawpaw. It can proliferate at least as far south as Melbourne and the North Island of New Zealand. It tolerates semi-shade and grows fast, fruiting within 10–14 months, adding instant tropicana to a garden. Few pests attack it. Provided that its distinct needs are met, it offers a lot.

It likes a lot of phosphorus, so put fertilisers such as blood-and-bone under its mulch.

Like avocados, it's susceptible to the water and soil transported fungi *Phytophora* so ensure good drainage. Plant it on a slope or make a half metre to one metre high mound. Heat can also knock it around, so shelter it from hot afternoon sun. Also protect it from wind as it's top heavy and can easily blow over.

The fruit is harvestable over three months and is ready to bring inside when about a third of it has turned yellow — at this stage they usually fall. I designed our garden so I can see the babacos lying at the base of the trees from the kitchen window.

To save money just buy one plant. Later the pruned stems can be chopped into 30-centimetre cuttings, left for 10 days in a cool area and then buried upright one third deep in potting mix. The cuttings will start growing quite quickly. These stems are plentiful as it helps to cut the plant back hard each year. Only allow one main stem to regrow.

Someday I think the babaco will gain the widespread appreciation its subtle but complex flavour deserves.

Chocolate Pudding Fruit
Diospyros digyna

You'd think its name alone would be alluring enough to boost sales in supermarkets; however, there's one boggy obstacle: it's only ready to eat when the olive skin shrivels and its flesh turns to mud-pie colour and consistency — brown and squishy.

Sadly, many gardening authors have scoffed at it as well. Perhaps their gastronomic palates melted in anticipation of full-bodied chocolate but then ran dry when they experienced a more subdued flavour. But mixed with yoghurt, vanilla

Don't go on looks — the chocolate pudding fruit may be soft, brown and squishy but each fruit has up to four times the vitamin C content of an orange.

and a touch of lemon juice or rum, this fruit becomes a bouncing chocolate mousse. It can also be converted into delicious ice cream, biscuits and bread.

Green globes of fruit swing for many months from the tree like drop-earrings, punctuating the shade beneath an arching canopy of emerald leaves. It's a marvellously shaped, tropical-looking tree, reaching about eight metres in height. And it doesn't demand a lot of attention — in fact, too much fertiliser can channel its vitality into burgeoning leaves at the expense of flowers and fruit. If you have the space, two trees will pollinate each other, enhancing the abundance of fruit. It prefers a tropical climate as well as warm temperate zones such as coastal New South Wales. If protected while young it handles some of the warmer pockets in Victoria. It tolerates 0°C when young and -2°C when older and hardier. The pulpy flesh is a clue, albeit somewhat remote, to its redskin relation — the persimmon — that survives much cooler conditions.

Feijoa
Feijoa sellowiana

The distinctive silver underside of the feijoa leaf is the hallmark of this tree's ornamental fame. Surprisingly, its fruit has generally been ignored and left to rot, as if decoration precluded flavour. In some instances this is justified as certain strains have been bred for appearance, not taste. Poor quality fruit also results from substandard seedlings. In successful ventures, however, the green, egg-shaped fruit is a delicious blend of passionfruit and pineapple. In fact its other name

Our feijoas grow beside a pathway so strollers can savour the novelty of the fleshy rose-flavoured petals.

The feijoa fruit looks quite dull, but it has a distinctive flavour which my neighbour and I wait for all year.

is pineapple guava. Other surprisingly palatable delights spring from the inventive pith of this tree: its fleshy rose-flavoured pink petals can be eaten without impacting on the impending fruit.

The feijoa produces abundantly. Last year we dried a great deal of its fruit with a plan for it to last us three months. They were too delicious for that — I polished off the lot in a few days.

It is one of the hardiest of all fruit trees and crops as far south as Tasmania, surviving -10°C. It fills out to be 5 metres wide, with an equivalent height. A line of them will, in time, spread into a good windbreak. The feijoa can live through wind and drought — but produces less fruit. It fruits optimally when well watered with good drainage and when plenty of fertiliser is applied.

A few books advise against growing it in fruit fly areas — but we can't resist. Some people go to the pub for entertainment — we bag the fruit on the feijoa trees.

Jaboticaba
Myrciaria cauliflora

Wine-tasting is one of the fastest growing tourism industries in Australia. Our district's climate is too humid to encourage large-scale production of grapes, yet somehow wine tourism has arisen. Many wineries have a token vineyard and then buy most of their wine elsewhere.

Perhaps some day our wine tourism will be based on a more relevant and tasty jaboticaba wine. It thrives here and its round, black fruit has a taste not unlike the muscat grape's. Yet the

Make sherbet-flavoured icy-balls by freezing jaboticabas.

People rarely get to see the elusive jaboticaba flowers and fruit as they are cauliferous (the flowers, not the people). That is, they grow directly out of the branches and are hidden by the leaves.

fruit can grow three times the size, with a zestier flavour. It makes a robust wine, following several glasses of which the word 'jaboticaba' seems to roll off the tongue with ease.

Its delicate leaves give this pretty 8-metre high tree a Japanese appearance. You'll need the patience of a Japanese tea ceremony as it grows slowly and may not fruit for over four years. Although the tree develops at tortoise pace, it makes up for lost time when it flowers, racing to fruit within 20–30 days and up to five times per year.

Jaboticabas grow faster if they're grafted, watered a lot, and grown in warmer climates — but not too hot. They can survive a light frost, and temperatures as low as -2°C when older. They produce fruit as far south as temperate areas, such as Sydney, but they need a sheltered micro-climate and can't tolerate cool climates. Pests rarely trouble them.

One bite and white translucent pulp bursts through. The skin is quite tough so chew everything and then spit it out with the pips.

Lemonade Fruit
Citrus limon var. *lemonade*

The name alone cajoles kids to eat and drink it. It's a sweet variety of lemon so when kids want a snack you can send them out to the tree to pluck the fruit and eat it in the garden. The bush looks similar to the conventional lemon, ensuring it's sweet taste is well disguised — until the neighbours' kids catch on.

This fruit is useful for making lemonade cordial without having to add teeth-chattering amounts of sugar. It's a cross between a Meyer lemon and a true lemon; Meyers are less acidic and sweeter than most lemons and could well be a lemon-orange hybrid. Lemonade fruits are much more rounded than a lemon, more orange-coloured and their skin is quite thin. This makes it more difficult to transport and store which is probably why it's difficult to find lemonades in the shops. Its thin skin also makes it more susceptible to fruit fly, although we have never had any in ours. The tree has had borers. The

Lemonade tree branches can break under the weight of all their fruit.

lemonade can tolerate colder weather and more frosts than other lemons as well as surviving the humidity of the tropics. The tree is quite small and bears prolifically from a young age and over a long period. The fruit is harvested mainly in autumn and winter.

Peanut Butter Tree
Bunchosia argentinia

The peanut butter tree is a novelty tree that doesn't produce a lot of food. A great way to fill conversation gaps at dinners is to test its flavour on friends.

Primarily, I bought the peanut butter tree so that Dean would no longer get upset when I bought smooth peanut butter instead of crunchy (or was it the other way around?).

It's an attractive small bushy tree with wavy leaves. The fruits ripen sporadically — usually through winter — turning yellow to orange to

No fizzer — the lemonade fruit is a refreshing change from oranges.

The peanut butter tree has dense evergreen foliage and is quite small, making it a conversation piece for urban areas.

The aptly named peanut butter fruits have no added sugar, salt or emulsifiers. The only question is — are they crunchy or smooth?

bright red. They taste best red, although by this time the pests start moving in so it is safer to eat them when they are orange-red. The plant is considered rare in Australia and I guess it originally came from South America (its botanic name hints at this). It can survive light frost and will grow as far south as the central coast of New South Wales.

Pepino
Solanum muricatum

This fruit looks like an elongated tennis ball, being a sallow yellow and striped with purple (see photo on page 150). Its taste is reminiscent of melon. It's not as fleshy but far easier to grow. It's a member of the tomato family and will prosper in most climates that foster tomatoes, if protected from frost. Some varieties have been developed with slight frost resistance and can grow as far south as Melbourne.

It's a versatile perennial plant, fruiting in its first year, but can be grown as an annual in cooler areas if the growing season is long enough. It reaches a metre high, and can grow in full sun among younger trees and then, when the giants dwarf little pepino, it flourishes as an understorey on a dappled stage. However, it fruits better in full sun, producing over a six-month period in good conditions. It lives up to three years.

We grow it in many locations but the plant that cascades over the rock wall fruits the most, probably due to the warmth of the wall. The fruits also keep longer if they're off the ground, so if you don't have a rock wall try growing them on a trellis.

Pepinos sprout readily from cuttings; one plant can be splintered into hundreds. Start with a specimen that has large and tasty fruit. A friend gave me a few cuttings from her fine fruiting specimen. It's so characteristic I can recognise other pepinos in the area that are derived from the same plant. It helps to replant cuttings every two years. They also grow well in pots.

Rose Apple
Syzygium jambos

Imagine eating the aromatic bliss of a rose.

Although we have a bouquet of rose apple trees, I've learnt to give visitors only mere morsels of the fruit so they can appreciate its

Surprisingly the showy rose-apple flower has no particular scent; the rose bouquet of the fruit makes up for this oversight.

Taste a rose apple and speculate where the idea for rose water originally came from.

flavour. Too much can be quite sickly. Distilled, the fruit makes first-grade rosewater.

Rose apples originated in Indonesia. They belong to the multi-faceted lilly pilly family and grow to about 8 metres. While they can survive in frost-free parts of Victoria, they fruit best in drier, cooler sub-tropical areas through to the warm humid tropics. Nurseries describe them as rare, although they grow easily from seed, true to type.

Tamarillo or Tree Tomato
Cyphomandra betacea

The lush 3-metre tall tamarillo bush has bountiful orange, red or yellow (which are sweeter) fruit. These dangle like Christmas tree baubles. Its flavour tends to excite passionate reactions — both venturesome and confused. It tastes like tomato mixed with passionfruit. As a fruit, people often expect a sweeter taste. As a salad vegetable, like the tomato, it's rarely eaten alone. They're ideal for creating salads that look like a work of art.

Tamarillo flowers — they must be fakes!

Blend the flesh with orange juice to make a Tamarillo Sunrise.

We find tamarillos add warm-coloured polka-dots to the garden. They're prodigious fruiters, with up to 15 kilograms per tree in less than two years. Since they fruit so quickly, they can be counted on while the other fruit trees catch up.

They grow from the tropics down to northern Tasmania, although they need to be positioned in a warm micro-climate, protected from frost. They tolerate some shade, so are a colourful way to highlight an area with limited sun. Plant successive crops for an ongoing supply as they only live for about four years.

White Sapote
Casimiroa edulis

If you adore the rich and creamy custard apple experience, but your area is too cold, then grow this delicious fruit. One of the most heavy producers of all fruit trees, it furnishes food in winter when stocks can be low. It fruits over a long period and so it's a good idea to have it in an area you look at regularly so you can pluck

them at the first wink of readiness. If you miss prime time, its fast and conspicuous (whiffy) fermenting process will remind you to keep a trained eye. (Some Brazilians apparently ferment them for alcohol to fuel their cars.)

Don't eat them before a long trip, unless you're the passenger. They are reputed to have a sedative effect. They're used for this in Mexico, as well as to reduce the pain of rheumatism and arthritis.

It is a large tree, reaching 10–15 metres wide and high. We situated it on the western side of a pathway to give us afternoon shade. I was hoping that after pruning it would allow us to walk underneath. However, its lateral limbs droop, and after four years, it's still not tall enough.

One of the best features of this little-known, tropical-looking tree is its ability to tolerate temperatures as low as -6°C. As it originated in the Mexican highlands, it fruits in regions as cold as Tasmania. It should be protected from hot afternoon summer sun, as this can burn new growth.

A creamy custard apple experience — even in cooler climates.

Vegetables and Herbs

Chilli
Capsicum spp.

Chillies conjure images of Asia although they have only been there for 400 years. They have been in Mexico much longer, where they became domesticated around 7000BC. They're not exactly a foreign plant to Australia either, yet few people grow them. You're unlikely to need many and in the meantime they are colourful ornamentals.

There are a number of different varieties, including purple and orange ones. They change colour, so it's a visual feast even if you don't like seeing them on your plate. Grow them where you can enjoy their artistry. They hang on the bush for a long time.

The chilli bush often self-seeds and its seedlings can be easily transplanted. It's often an annual in cooler climates. Alternatively, if you grow it in a

A perennial chilli capsicum with bite. Kids are only seduced by its bright colours once.

The flowers of the chilli capsicum bush advertise the up-coming show.

pot in a sheltered position or take it inside, this will increase its chance of becoming a perennial.

The chilli's taste ranges from mild to dynamite, depending on the amount of capsaicin present in the variety. Hot chillies can be a problem with young kids, though chillies tend to teach their lessons well and fast. If the kids are caught out, don't reach for water as capsaicin is water insoluble (like oil) and water will not quell the burning — bananas, rice, potato and dairy products, such as yoghurt, pacify the fire.

Surprisingly, the heat from capsaicin cools down the body in hot weather. The blood vessels dilate to increase circulation and encourage perspiration.

Chooks often love them, although I sometimes think roosters can't handle them so well — that's why they crow incessantly.

River-like veins of the cocoyam leaves catch flowers and rainbow sparkles.

Cocoyam
Xanthosoma sagittifolium

Gazing down from the veranda, the 1-metre heart-shaped leaves of the cocoyam spread out laterally, as if on display. Delicate white flowers flutter down from the male pawpaw above, landing on the leaves.

We grow these because they look so tropical and they have a wonderful symmetry when looked on from above. They thrive in moist parts of the garden producing tubers that are creamier than potatoes and similarly nutritious. As they're perennial we don't need to replant them, we simply ferret around their edges for the tubers. We've learned to restrain our excesses with ferreting, so the plant doesn't fall over.

The cocoyam will prevail over a vegetable garden, so it is better suited further afield in a clean, moist area. Plant the central tuberous root (corm). After three months it will be surrounded by smaller tubers (cormels). These span a comparable size range to potatoes. The cormels can be eaten boiled, roasted or mashed. When mashed they need only a small addition of butter and milk, as they're naturally smooth and creamy. A squeeze of lemon heightens the flavour.

The tender young leaves and shoots can also be eaten — cooked and used like spinach. It grows well in light shade. It originated in the tropics but can grow in warm micro-climates in temperate areas, although the cormels will take longer to grow and will be smaller.

Cocoyam corms: an easy-to-grow and creamy alternative to mashed potato.

Curry Leaf Tree
Murraya koenigii

Once some apprehensive Indians, who hadn't been in the country long, visited us. They looked displaced and uncomfortable. Then they saw our curry tree. They raised their voices and excitement bubbled: now we were on the same wavelength.

Northern Indians rely on mint in their cuisine, while in the south they depend on the pungent curry leaves. Many families grow them, even in pots if they have little space. In the early stages of a curry, they fry about fifteen of its small leaves along with spices, such as mustard seeds and cumin. This flavouring then emanates through the curry, giving it a lingering aroma. Before serving the curry the leaves are usually taken out. An old Indian saying likens people who are used and then discarded to the fate of a curry leaf.

Throw out the curry powder and experience the authentic taste of the curry leaf tree.

We planted this bushy 3-metre tree near the big round window at the entrance to our house. This prevents curiosity merchants from peering in. Being so close, we can easily furnish the indigenous requirements for a curry. Fresh leaves are difficult to buy. While cooked leaves lend a potent flavour to a curry they smell a bit strong on the bush for some people.

In areas with a cold winter it can be grown in pots in a sheltered area or greenhouse; where summers are hot, it's best grown in dappled shade. It can become rampant in some climates; if this could be a problem for you then either plant it in quite a harsh position or in a pot. Ours is planted in quite a dry area so that it doesn't send up lots of suckers — just a few to give to friends.

Jerusalem Artichoke
Helianthus tuberosus

This is one of the easiest edible plants to grow, and is relatively pest resistant. In sixteenth-century Italy Jerusalem artichokes were made into alcohol for the soldiers.

Leave this herbaceous perennial in a forgotten part of the garden and it will toil and multiply. It grows in most soil but prefers fertile, sandy soil. It's hardy throughout a lot of Australia, yet in areas such as Victoria it tends to become a weed if not managed well. To increase its yield of tubers, cut off the flowers (and put them in a vase). Harvest the tubers in autumn. Store some in dry sand to plant the following season.

Jerusalem artichokes can be grated in salads, boiled or baked. Fried with garlic, then pureed with chicken stock and finished with a dollop of cream, they make a delicious soup. They are used to promote lactation and are recommended for diabetics.

Kaffir Lime
Citrus hystrix

Ours grows near the drive, so I can pluck a handful of leaves before a long drive and stay awake by inhaling its refreshing aroma. It's not grown for its small, knobbly fruit; rather for its leaves that can be harvested year-round. It's helpful to grow this near the kitchen door as two or three of its leaves are essential for some authentic Thai dishes. Few bottled Thai curry pastes capture the flavour of freshly picked kaffir lime leaves.

Try adding shredded leaves to salad and roasted vegies — and use it to flavour soy sauce. It's a citrus but no other member of the citrus family gives such a tangy bouquet, except perhaps the native finger lime.

The kaffir lime grows about 4 metres tall and belongs to the same genus as lemons and oranges. It is thought to have originated in Asia and traditionally people grow them near their houses as they are believed to ward off evil spirits. Cultivate them like other citruses — plant in well-drained soil, water in dry times, mulch them well and give them plenty of nutrients, even seaweed foliar sprays. If it is looking pale feed it iron chelate annually.

Waft into Thailand on the smell of a kaffir lime leaf.

It has a unique, appealing look. The leaves double-up — a leaf grows on the end of each leaf. It can grow in the tropics and sub-tropics and in warm temperate areas in a beneficial micro-climate, such as in a pot against a warm wall. It may need to be brought into a more sheltered position in winter.

Quite a few local people planted commercial quantities and are making good money as its popularity increases.

Lebanese Cress
Aethionema curdifolum

I often wondered how this lush and leafy green could originate from the Mediterranean area. It seemed more like a tropical Asian green. Then I saw it growing alongside a shady creek in Jordan in a region that gets heavy snow falls. It was rampant there — as it is in a section of our vegie garden. It wasn't a good idea to grow it with the vegetables — although with double cardboard surrounding it, we've managed to restrain it to about a square metre.

As it's so hardy, it could be in a less prime spot — such as an area that catches clean water run off. However, I do like it close by as we use it regularly in salads. I enjoy it for its subtle carroty flavour, not quite the case with its namesake — cress.

Easy-to-grow Lebanese cress gives a carrot flavour all year round.

Lotus
Nelumbo nucifera

The lotus grows in naturally permanent lagoons, an environment which can be easily simulated by planting it in full sun in a sunken bathtub or in a pond (in a container if need be). It can go rampant in a dam and cost a packet to remove. It prefers 10–15 centimetres of water and nutrient-rich soil: one part rotted cow manure; four parts soil; a cup of blood and bone; and some wood ash. It grows in large pots as an ornamental.

Plant in early spring for best results. It grows from the tropics down, with cold-tolerant varieties growing as far south as Tasmania. Here they benefit from a lot of sun and wind-protection when young.

The enormous round leaves and mainly pink, white or yellow flowers often protrude as high as a metre out of the water. The flowers are 25-centimetres wide and have a subtle, yet exquisite aroma. They are stunning as cut flowers — but don't make the mistake of using them as decoration for a wedding: they only last a few hours, then droop horribly. If picked before they open they will last longer. The dried seedpods endure for ages and look intriguing in floral arrangements.

Aborigines use many parts of the lotus. They roast the seeds, the inside of the leaf stems and the roots.

A cross-section of the root displays a mandala pattern. It absorbs the flavour of

All eyes are on the edible lotus seeds.

stronger food, while maintaining its shape. In Asia, the immature leaves are eaten fresh as a vegetable or boiled and added to stir-fries. The seeds may be eaten young as fresh green peas. The older ones are eaten raw, like peanuts, or boiled in stews. The petals give artistic inspiration to a salad and the tubers can be eaten raw like an apple, although they are slightly astringent. To make lotus-root coffee — slice, roast and grind the root.

All parts of the lotus are used in Chinese herbal medicine. Its ability to furnish a beautiful pristine-white symmetry from the blackest of chaotic bogs makes it a universal symbol for the divine ability within us all to transform darkness into light.

Mushroom Plant
Rungia klossii

Imagine a leafy plant that tastes like mushroom. It's a playful trick to fool friends. Ours grows under a deciduous umbrella-shaped tree, where it's partly shaded in summer and receives full sun in winter. And it loves it. Despite my continual plucking, it has been growing voluminously for four years. It keeps on surprising me, especially since it rarely gets watered or nurtured. We put it in salads or stir-fries when we haven't got mushrooms. It doesn't have the same pulpy texture — but other vegies can compensate for that. It's great for mushroom-flavoured stocks.

It's one of the main tropical vegetables of Papua New Guinea and thrives from hot through to warm temperate areas. It would probably grow as an annual in cooler areas.

Society Garlic
Fulbaghia violacea

If you like garlic and are trying to get pregnant, follow this ancient prescription: use the less potent society garlic leaves as a substitute — then your partner will be able to get close enough for you to conceive.

The society garlic's leaves look like miniature iris leaves and it has delicate purple flowers swirling around like a ballerina's dress. It's easily divided and makes an effective edge to the vegetable garden as well as decorating a flower garden. Its stems, leaves and flowers are eaten, becoming less potent when lightly cooked. It grows from cool temperate areas through to the sub-tropics.

The delicate lilac flowers of the society garlic add softness to a garden edge.

Yucon
(Sweet Fruit Root)
Polymnia sonchifolia

This ancient-looking plant originated in South America. It was so popular it was even found in pre-Inca tombs. After this initial popularity it became quite rare. For all that, it's tastier, easier to grow and suffers less from pests than various modern, genetically modified foods. In Australia it's still relatively unknown.

Not for long, however. Soon restaurateurs will seize upon this crunchy apple-and-carrot-flavoured root, calling it a gourmet specialty food. Then the public will agree that it has an excellent taste. When people see how to use it raw as a sweet fruit, or cooked as a savoury vegetable, it may become part of everyday cuisine.

It can be sliced to scoop up dips and as a substitute for biscuits — with something flavoursome on top. It's a great staple — without the dreary taste often associated with staples.

Growing around the yucon stem is the cluster of rhizomes, which are different to and much smaller than the tasty edible tuber. Only buy one and over the years create hundreds of plants.

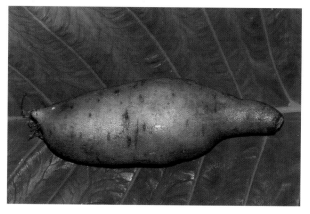

Although the yucon tuber looks like a sweet potato, it's not starchy. It has the taste and crunch of a carroty apple.

This 1.5-metre tall bush can grow in most areas of mainland Australia. The suprisingly small yellow daisy flowers are in sharp contrast to its huge arrow-shaped furry leaves, somewhat reminiscent of a scene from *The Day of the Triffids*. It's easier to grow than potatoes and attracts fewer pests. Amazingly, it doesn't need full sun, so it's a great filler plant in more shady areas of the garden with dappled shade provided it is given enough height to grow. If the corms are planted about 80 centimetres apart, they'll rebuff the competition of weeds.

In five months, start fossicking for the tubers that grow out from the base of the plant. Continue

The hardy yucon grows vigorously in sun and dappled shade.

with this for another three months. Then dig up the whole plant and collect all the tubers, which can grow up to 40 centimetres long and weigh as much as 2 kilograms each. They'll sweeten further if left in the sun for about four days. They store well in a dark cupboard or in a bucket of moist sand. Commercially they can yield 38 tonnes per hectare.

We save many rhizomes to give to friends. Each plant yields up to 20 rhizomes. These are then planted out in spring or whenever they start to grow naturally. The plants have been selling for as much as $15 each. Now there are enough people sharing the rhizomes, the price should drop quickly.

Sweet Leaf Bush
Sauropus androgynus

I saw this growing prolifically along degraded and polluted roadsides in Vietnam. It's tough. It has been flourishing beneath the eaves of our house for three years, despite receiving little water, and it's only starting to slow down now. It grows to about 3 metres in a wide range of soils and thrives in both sun and dappled shade. Frost can affect it, yet sometimes after a heavy frost it reshoots from the ground.

It has attractive tiny red fruit but it is the oval green leaves that are eaten, two months after planting. They taste like fresh peas. They're high in protein weighing in at a massive 34%. It gives the flavour we want when peas are out of season — and is less work. The young leaves are thin and delicate — it would take a true princess to detect them under a mattress.

Vietnamese Mint
Persicaria odorata

Vietnamese mint has a strong, hot peppery flavour, so add at the last minute to curries and stir-fries. It gives a terrific zest to salads.

It's easy to raise from cuttings and seed, growing 60-centimetres tall. It's a perennial in warm regions and an annual in cold regions, although this can be extended if it's brought inside in winter. It won't tolerate frosts. Grow it in shade or semi-shade.

It grows prolifically in South-East Asia in moist areas. It's actually not a true mint, although it does exhibit its rampant characteristics in fertile conditions. Be cautious with Vietnamese mint as it can't be shaded out and so can become rampant in shady areas. For safety, grow it in a pot.

With a distinctive peppery flavour, the Vietnamese mint adds zest to many Asian dishes, including Vietnamese spring rolls.

The water chestnut plants turn our black bog into white coconut-flavoured crunch.

Dean and his daughter Erin try a bit of mud wrestling. You only need to wrestle out a few water chestnuts to get a free facial mud mask.

The difference between canned and fresh water chestnuts is like the difference between powdered and fresh ginger.

Water Chestnut
Eleocharis dulcis

Once I was on national television grovelling in thigh-high mud in a drained dam. No it wasn't a slap-stick venture into sitcoms; this program was about the harvesting of commercially grown water chestnuts. Now I grovel through my own mud-filled bathtubs instead.

Decent water chestnuts are at least the diameter of a 20-cent coin. They're arduous to peel, so it's a good job to do when you've plenty of friends to lend a hand or when listening to the radio. They taste like mellow coconut and add a unique crunchy texture to a meal.

Water chestnuts are grown commercially in Victoria, New South Wales, Queensland and the Northern Territory. They have a delicate flavour for such a hardy plant. Fortunately they don't need any watering or weeding. In early spring, plant them into about 40 centimetres of rich soil in a bathtub or container at the rate of about two per square metre. Ensure any fertiliser is well broken down and integrated, otherwise it will turn into a smelly liquid fertiliser. Keep the soil moist until the shoots are about 10 centimetres high. Then flood until the water reaches the top of the shoot tips. As the plant grows taller, continue to add more water in, until it reaches about 20–40 centimetres. Then let it grow out of the water. After about seven frost-free months, the reeds will start to dry out and die. Don't panic. Drain the water, take the dead vegetation away and leave the chestnuts in the tub for about one more month. Frost will help sweeten them. Harvest and keep them unpeeled for up to a month in the fridge.

When we were first growing them some free blood and bone hopped into the tub and drowned: cane toads. What a stink. We took the hint and put in some frog logs, so visitors can now jump out.

Bush Foods

My sister Juliet and I once ventured into isolated bush to see how long we could survive just on the food we found. Having finished a double major in politics I felt eager to take on the world. The world, however, wasn't so eager to give itself up.

Day 1: We built a bark overhang and, in gastronomic anticipation, made a wombat trap. We caught a small fish. Day 2: We ate gnarly old tree roots. We used up more energy digging them than we extracted from them. Day 3: A yabbie. Day 4: Juliet entertained a small lizard while I snuck up behind it and macheted its head off. It only had a morsel of meat in its tail and I'm sure Juliet got the bigger half. Day 5: A meat pie, three sausage rolls and a chocolate milkshake captured with our bare hands by simply fluttering a bit of paper as bait to the shopkeeper.

Since realising how difficult it is to live on bush foods, I've studied them more. I also believe this is an important part of understanding and respecting Aboriginal culture. Burke and Wills might have wished they had. They starved in an area where Aborigines thrived. Our native bush foods have a lot to offer, yet it is up to us to understand their unique flavours, so that we can use them to complement present-day cuisine.

Often people equate harvesting bush foods with wrestling crocodiles, Mick Dundee style. For your own bush food adventure, with a touch less peril, try growing an exciting array of edible native plants throughout the garden.

Aniseed Myrtle
Backhousia anisata

As I write this, I'm sipping a cup of aniseed myrtle tea. The cysanathol in its leaves makes some people slightly euphoric, yet all I feel is pleasantly numb lips. However, I do feel refreshed and stimulated to keep writing.

Although it's a stunning rainforest tree, few aniseed myrtles still exist in their natural habitat around Bellingen, northern New South Wales. Many landholders cleared them. Fortunately, many now realise the opportunities in the bush-food industry and are clearing fewer of them. There's an understanding in the bush-food industry that only a particular percentage of leaves or fruit is to be taken from specific native plants, depending on the species and its age. The

When Australia overcomes its cultural food cringe, aniseed myrtle may make it up there in the culinary pantheon with licorice and cinnamon.

problem occurs when five separate groups do this in one week.

Under cultivation, the aniseed myrtle reaches a bushy 6 metres. It takes about three to five years before it's commercially productive. It enjoys full sun, tolerates a light frost and works well in a windbreak. It has bright burgundy new growth and its undulating leaves make it ornamental and a great pot specimen.

It's brilliant for flavouring biscuits, desserts and sauces. Kids love eating the young leaves, a healthy alternative to humbugs.

Davidson's Plum
Davidsonia pruriens
var. *jerseyana*

Only the brave eat them straight. This plum is tart, with three times the acidity of a blood plum. The tartness needs to be worked with strategically to highlight its unique flavour in an acceptable way. It goes particularly well in sauces, jams and wine and can often be substituted in recipes for plums (use a third as many).

The tree is quite rare in its natural habitat in and around the rainforests of north-eastern New South Wales. It grows to about 4–6 metres with a stunning leaf-display that swirls outwards from a central stem. It needs to be protected from extreme heat and frost. It can also be grown further south. It thrives in both the Sydney and Melbourne Botanic Gardens, although I imagine it fruits less.

We planted three below the balcony so we could look down on their delightful maroon growth shooting out the top. Yet one just

While savouring delicious Davidson's plum jam we should thank the maligned fruit bat for its careful cross-pollination and selection over the millennia.

wouldn't stop growing, like a prop for *Jack and the Beanstalk*. It has already reached 8 metres and is still going strong, unfortunately dividing our view in two. (We've just discovered this one is the taller North Queensland variety — *Davidsonia pruriens* var. *pruriens*.)

The 5-centimetre dark purple plums are cauliferous — they grow directly on the trunk or branches. It makes a stunning pot plant. Put it somewhere guests won't be tempted to caress it: its Latin name, *pruriens*, means itchy, but it's not that problematic.

Lemon-scented Myrtle
Backhousia citriodora

A cup of lemon myrtle tea is exquisitely refreshing. It's such a good cleanser that a friend visits us merely for a cup of tea — he then feels he can justify another cigarette.

Since it has a more intense favour than lemon grass, with about eight times its citral content, it's becoming popular in Asian dishes. It grows rapidly, reaching 3–10-metres, and enjoys full sun. It prefers to be protected from wind. In many cases it can cope with poorly drained soil, although it relishes well-drained soil with plenty of watering. It can tolerate slight frosts, even though it's quite tender when young. It grows well here, while cooler climes, such as the Melbourne Botanic Gardens and the Blue Mountains, tend to slow it down a bit. It attracts birds and butterflies and looks good as a pot ornamental. Ours are planted along the edges of paths so people get a sense of something uplifting in the wind as they brush past.

In the tea section of the garden supermarket, lemon-scented myrtle leaves advertise their refreshing flavour every time we brush past them in the aisle.

Macadamia Nut
Macadamia integrifolia

Early Australian agriculturalists overlooked this scrumptious native nut. As a result, the macadamia went to Hawaii to be produced on a commercial scale at the turn of the last century. Sixty years later, Australia caught on and brought it back because it bought the marketing hype.

Despite being an Australian native, many forms now carry Hawaiian names and some of its best crops are grown in Hawaii. A few of their selections will not completely adapt back to less tropical Australian conditions.

It grows well north to the Atherton Tablelands and south to Hobart, tolerating -6°C. If you have the space, it's better to grow more than one tree, as they crop better with cross-pollination.

The nut is a member of the protea family. Like its colourful cousins the waratahs, grevilleas and banksias, the macadamia is adapted to low levels of phosphorus. If you have natives in the garden, especially members of this family, be careful not to give them too much phosphorus.

The dense macadamia tree grows to about 10 metres. It prospers in most good soils and it can handle some shade, as it naturally grows as an understorey tree in rainforests. It's fairly drought-resistant but produces better with good irrigation, especially around spring and early summer. Its optimal conditions include protection from harsh winds and frost and being open to full sun. In hot areas the bark on the younger trees can scorch in the sun.

It should produce after about four years. In 10 years it can yield 25 kilograms of nuts in a season. Some success stories claim a production rate of up to 100 kilograms. It reaches its maximum productivity at around 20 years.

Macadamias are rich in oil, sugar and protein and, encased in such a tough shell, you would think they could rebuff most marauding animals — bush rats, however, can gnaw through the tough shell. The tree attracts birds, butterflies and many varieties of humans. It supplies the body with megawatts of energy — enough to go and plant more of this abundant tree.

The small-leaved lilly pilly's bright pink young leaves make it a feature tree.

Small-leaved Lilly Pilly
Syzygium leuhmannii

This lilly pilly bears a spicy fruit, which tastes like a zingy blend of ginger and cinnamon. As it's such a festive tree, decking itself with sprays of young pink foliage, it makes a wonderful display along a path. It's a popular street and screen tree in Brisbane and Sydney and grows well in the west and along most of the eastern seaboard, including the Blue Mountains. The blue lilly pilly and common lilly pilly thrive more in the south.

Growing 5–10 metres tall, this species attracts birds, is a good windbreak, works as a fire retardant in a fire break, and flourishes along creek banks, where its spreading root system binds the soil and helps control erosion.

It prefers well-drained soil and can grow in both full sun and part shade, although it will fruit best in the former. It's not frost tolerant when young. Aim for trees with fruit that is seedless or has small seeds. It fruits within three to four years. The most promising report is of 60 kilograms of fruit harvested from one tree in one season.

Being so attractive, the small-leaved lilly pilly has reached the top echelons of society by decorating the main street in Noosa. It fruits well there in the well-drained soil and pleasant coastal conditions. One year, thousands of the fruit were hanging from the tree and falling on the footpath. Concerned with the imminent danger of Noosa's white sandshoes becoming mercilessly stained, we disarmed some of the tree (leaving a substantial amount, as is the norm). Dressed as we were, the Noosaites probably took us for local council and didn't seem to mind. We sold enough to cover the tab on a few Noosa meals.

Warrigal Greens
Tetragonia tetragonoides

Growing wild in every state of Australia, Warrigal greens are a great substitute for European spinach. In many cases, too, they're easier to grow. We stumbled across an enormous amount that was tumbling out of a seaside garden. So we filled up the back of the ute, sold some to a restaurant ($16 per box) and froze the rest. By the end of eating this it did remind me of the dreaded frozen spinach from my younger days, but without the added bits of extra protein — slugs.

Although it's believed not to have been eaten by Aborigines, it was eat greens or die with Captain Cook and his crew when they arrived in Botany Bay. They needed it to resist scurvy. They were so pleased with it they took it back to Kew Gardens in London in 1771.

Since then it has become naturalised in California, Chile, China and Natal in South Africa

For a taste of Australia's Warrigal greens go to a restaurant in Europe — or save the airfare and grow your own.

where the Zulus eat it regularly. Early last century, it was fashionable in Europe as a summer spinach. It's now the most popular native Australian vegetable to be consumed overseas. Maybe we'll have to wait for America to sell it to us. Until that day, few Australians are likely to know about it.

It's a useful plant as it grows in both sun and semi-shade, although more prolifically in the former. I let it sprawl underneath the fruit trees as a groundcover. Conveniently, it reseeds itself so the supply is endless, although it slows after an initial burst of enthusiasm in the first year. It grows as an annual in cool climates.

Warrigal greens can be grown from seeds or cuttings. It needs a good supply of nitrogen to support its leafy habit. It survives frost to -3°C.

You can eat the new stem, the leaves and 5 centimetres of the growing tips. It contains calcium oxalates, which need to be removed by blanching. Don't reuse this water. Apparently, better tasting low-oxalate forms are being developed in Europe. Again, this Aussie native's potential is being maximised overseas. Soon it may be marketed as a European product.

To bring the thrill of harvesting exciting food closer to reality, you could either emulate my sister's and my bush-food experience, learn to live in the bush properly or see page 241 for a list of quality nurseries and seed sources. Your local nurseries may sell them as well. Buy carefully. Some nurseries promote the stock that they want to move out the door fastest. This isn't necessarily the best for you.

The next chapter shows techniques for buying well, so you can be sure you are getting the best quality advice and materials.

Avoid
Seduction

The ancient story of the wooden horse that was built

to capture Troy shows how the power of seduction

led to the downfall of a civilisation. If unprepared,

seduction can have a similar effect on the garden. Be

aware and buy smartly; avoid being duped.

The heart of a bird's nest fern.

Seduction steals up on you when you least expect it. On the way home from work you race into the supermarket for the bare essentials. You reach the checkout counter, flushed with contentment because you've stuck to the shopping list, fighting off the chocolatey temptations. Then a pot of bright blue flowers smiles sweetly at you, highlighted by spotlights, almost dancing to the upbeat music. Unknown to you, it's a rampant weed. Yet its glitzy label, bigger than itself, conjures images of your dream garden. Suddenly, you miss a heartbeat — it's on special for this week only. Can you let this opportunity go?

Never ask of money spent...

Robert Frost

Probably not. Supermarkets, and many other sales outlets, are skilfully engineered to break people away from the routine of their shopping lists, and give in to their impulses.

Resistance is futile, or hard work. It gets tricky to know what's what as the options multiply. The availability of plants used to be limited to mainly nurseries, markets and fetes. Now they're sold in a range of unlikely outlets, such as petrol stations, primarily because they have the marketing power. They're in a position to seduce when the protective shield is down. But buying a fruit tree from the petrol station can be like getting a haircut at the hardware store. There is no expertise and the standard will be variable. In both cases, it's difficult to return a fortnight later for a refund.

The art of seduction is more about what it hides than what it reveals.

Smart Buying

Shopping for plants influences the garden's character *and* genetic stock; and the effects can continue for generations. So if you have the time and energy it's worth taking the steps to do it well.

There are Washington Navels and there are Washington Navels.

Franz Honnef (Honnef's Fruit and Nut Tree Nursery)

STEP 1: Enter the shopping arena resolved to defy emotional seduction. Make a reconnaissance trip around a range of well-stocked nurseries to gather information, check out the stock and see what needs to be considered. Resisting temptation, such as a chocolate pudding fruit tree, may be difficult, so ease the tension by leaving your credit card and chequebook at home (and enjoy the consumer-release feeling). Ask for catalogues and plant lists. Take them home to peruse with a relaxing cup of tea.

If you don't have the time for browsing, try to organise for potential nurseries to send their catalogue to you — it helps if they have good descriptions.

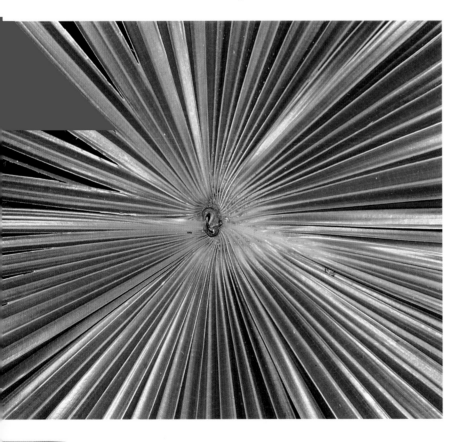

A cabbage tree palm frond.

The coastal banksia flower.

STEP 2: With an informed opinion of the plants, walk around your garden and visualise them as mature specimens in different areas — an imaginative friend can help. This is a good time to decide what species you want and, more specifically, to distinguish between their varieties. For example, you can buy avocado varieties that are propagated onto stock that is more resistant to the fungus *Phytophora*. Or, if you only have room for one pecan nut tree, look for a variety that is self-pollinating.

STEP 3: Now you're ready for that special occasion — a shopping spree at the nurseries, plastic card to the fore. To avoid getting flustered, try to choose a day with good weather and a time when it won't be making you too hot, or late for another appointment. If you don't have your own list of species and varieties to hand, at least have an idea of the niches you want to fill, so you don't come back with five prickly rosebushes to grow around the kids' ball area. Oh and enjoy!

Having said that, impulse buying does have some advantages. It maximises opportunities and can be inspirational. If you must be seduced, ensure you buy plants that are non-rampant and can readily be accommodated into your garden, such as herbs, flowers and 1-metre filler bushes.

I once bought a pine swinging-chair from an agricultural show. It was a rash move. Two years later, two kids were swinging in it when it collapsed under them. Its joints had rotted. It's now too late to track down the merchants to hold them accountable. Transience means it's easier to get away with fobbing off inferior goods. Or maybe I'm the one who should be held accountable — I was duped into buying it.

We invited an experienced local carpenter to create our next swinging-chair, out of hardwood timber. It should last over 15 years. And I know where he lives.

My advice to anybody buying for their garden is to buy from specialist outlets with an accredited history. Well-established businesses with a proven track record and premises you can visit offer the best prospects. For example, I buy most of my native plants from our local Landcare nursery that has been running for over 10 years. To add more colourful natives, I visit a nursery which was converted from an old sugar cane plantation nearly 20 years ago and now has the largest selection of natives in south-eastern Queensland. Many of the species they sell also grow on-site, so I can see how the mature plant sizes up, helping keep things in perspective. They've selected for strong genetic stock and they recognise what will dangerously proliferate like a weed. Knowledgeable information is part of the service.

A nursery's ethics are detectable at a glance. Do they fob off weeds as garden plants? Do they sell plants that won't grow in your area? Are they offering certain vegetable seedlings when it is too late in the season to plant them? I saw one petrol station-cum-nursery selling eggplants as winter

Native violets.

We bought this pawpaw plant from a fruit tree nursery that has many of the parent species growing on-site..

A Fertile Rapport

approached and asked the sales assistant why. Laughing, he replied, 'They're leftovers — if people are stupid enough to buy them, that's their problem. And it means they'll come back to buy more plants to replace the dead ones.'

Check the nursery is vigilant about keeping weeds out of seedling pots. Wander out the back to see whether they're potting up in dirty or unsterilised pots, potentially spreading diseases such as *Phytophora cinnamomi*. Phytophora is a cinnamon-coloured fungus that spreads by soil and water, and attacks a plant's root system. The roots start to die off and then so does the top of the plant. This is the most deadly of all root diseases and kills 10% of Australia's avocado trees. The best nurseries have stock that is certified as disease free. It's well worth it.

After evaluating your best quality outlets, it helps to establish a healthy rapport with a reliable and knowledgeable salesperson who understands the subtleties of their stock.

Before visiting my favourite fruit and nut tree nursery, I make a time to see the owners. That way I can get specific and relevant advice without interruption. The nursery has been experimenting with fruit and nut trees for 27 years and know their different flavours. They've been building up strong genetic stock and can answer questions about even the most obscure varieties, as well as being able to detail the particulars of new stock. It's a win-win situation. I'm seduced by their juicy descriptions of fruits and they recycle my money.

Buying from businesses that offer valuable and supportive information ensures good value for money. For example, the owners of the organic

Cultivate a weed-free mulch man.

Picking the Healthiest Stock

Many nurseries sell robust stock. The ones who don't are either badly managed or simply profiteering.

In the wild, less than 1% of plants germinate and grow to maturity — it is survival of the fittest, and the weak and sick plants that cannot compete die. In some nurseries more than 90% of plants germinate and mature. But this does not mean that these plants are genetically strong. With such a discrepancy between nature and the nursery, chances are you're buying weak genetics. Some unhealthy plants might be nurtured back to vigour, but it's rarely worth the trouble and risk.

Look for healthy new growth.

mail order supplier Green Harvest have cultivated a blooming science of organic growing, with an eye to integrated pest management. They send useful information sheets with many purchases and answer specific questions about stock by phone. There aren't many people of their calibre running a mail order business.

My mulch man is also very welcoming. Over a cup of tea he defines his farming techniques and the advantages of his latest crops. I feel confident he won't sell weed-infested mulch.

Entrepreneurs who don't familiarise themselves with the science of their products inadvertently reveal themselves. A component of my research for this book was to analyse fruit trees on sale at petrol stations. I happened to mention to the cashier that I didn't think one variety they offered would grow well in our area. He didn't want to know. To avoid the topic he grabbed a red rose from the sales bucket and shoved it in my face telling me it was 'left over' from Valentine's Day. Perhaps if I went back every day with a bit of advice I could have collected a nice mixed bunch by the end of the week.

Here is a list of things to look for when buying plants.

Ensure the plant will achieve the purpose for which you intend it. For example, if you want a bushy plant, choose one that is already showing those traits above the others in the batch.

Look for strength in the stem or trunk. Don't choose spindly or leggy specimens. Avoid seedlings that divide down low and may split at the junction when they grow older.

Choose plants that have fresh new tip growth.

Leaves should be clean and free from insects, diseases or stress. Check for sap-sucking insects on the trunk.

Look for good colour in the leaves, not yellow, washed out or faded.

Weeds growing in the pot are an indication of bad nursery hygiene.

Do a bit of research to try to predict a given plant's productivity. For example, many fruit trees are grafted to root stock from a tree that is known to consistently produce high-quality fruit. Buying a similar plant as a seedling, however, is far less predictable, and could takes years to show itself as a poor fruiter.

We bought this giant laulau as a vigorous seedling and it hasn't looked back.

Make sure the roots are in balance with the overall size of the plant and are not root bound. Do not buy plants whose roots are growing out of the pot's drainage holes.

In an attempt to get the best value don't automatically select the tallest plants. Larger plants in nurseries have often been re-potted many times and their roots may have formed into a ball. This can be detrimental for long-term plant vigour and production. Plants in smaller pots have had less time to adapt to pot culture (they weren't brought up in the 70s) and will often respond quicker in the ground than older, larger ones. This is particularly important for fruit or large trees, especially those with a long tap root that needs to grow directly down into the soil for plant stability and quality.

Transporting stock home carefully is crucial. To avoid windburn in the back of open vans or trailers, lie large plants down and cover everything with a tarpaulin. Wrap the pots in plastic bags so that the soil remains with the roots. Drive conservatively so the plants don't get knocked around or shocked. If you don't have appropriate transport, consider having them delivered. To help them overcome stress offer them a drink on arrival.

Selecting accessories can be as demanding as buying plants. Buyer beware. It's so easy to forget the contingent requirements, panic at the last minute and grab an inferior product. This is often the case with mulch. Gardeners, realising their plot is urgently crying out for it, often flick through the local papers and find it offered cheaply. No name given, just a telephone number. It arrives quickly and is scattered in haste. Several weeks later a blanket of weeds raises its ugly head, haunting the garden for years to come. The sales people respond by saying they never guaranteed it to be weed-free... and they're right.

We bought this palm when it was just in a tube and planted it in a moist, well-prepared part of the garden. Unlike many plants in larger pots, it took off immediately and hasn't looked back.

Money-savers

*I*f your wallet's feeling as defoliated as an apricot in winter, here are some tips that can help maintain those salad days.

Ruby Red chard grows vigorously. Only grow as much food as you and your friends really want.

Nurseries

Nurseries regularly offer a healthy discount, if you spend a healthy amount. By planning ahead you can buy all your items on the one day to reach the target amount. If you're getting close but can't quite make it, buy birthday presents. You can never go wrong with quality secateurs. Maybe pool with a friend so together you can reach the stipulated amount. Or, if you have a friend in the gardening business, shop alongside them where they get significant discounts.

If a nursery doesn't publicly offer a discount and you know you will be spending big, don't be shy to ask about one. They will usually agree to cut their profits rather than lose the sale. Or, if you've seen materials sold cheaper elsewhere but are unable to reach the location, they may be persuaded to match the price.

Some punnets of seedlings hold more than can be eaten by the average family. So rather than planting out 16 silverbeet and force-feeding the kids, share densely planted punnets with a friend. Some nurseries or market stalls allow you to select the number of vegetable seedlings of each variety you want.

Try buying more expensive plants from wholesale nurseries. You can save if you're willing to forsake service and are happy to buy multiples of one species — perhaps six of each, and plants without tags — although they may put a tag on one representative of each species. If you know what you want, you may be able to fax them ahead or at least let them know when you're coming in, so you get reasonable attention.

If you really want expensive plants and lots of them, buy types that can be multiplied by cuttings, seeds or root division. This way you only need to buy one or two of each variety. Cultivate a section of your garden thoroughly for plants intended for division and replanting in the rest of the garden.

Filler plants are plants that can be used to fill empty or drab spaces in your garden. They also tend to be the plants that blow the budget so it helps to restrict your choice to ones that can be

If you don't want to replant all the pumpkin seeds, they're delicious fried with tamari.

multiplied by division or cutting. Or a potted groundcover that roots at sundry points, for example, may be taken out, then cut lengthwise in half and made into two plants.

Non-hybrid vegetable and herb seeds reproduce more predictable offspring. If you buy these you can select for robust genes by gathering seeds from your healthiest plants that highlight the traits you desire (for example, pest resistance or flavour). This is genetic adaptation along the lines nature intended.

Mulch

Come to an arrangement with your mulch supplier whereby you find them clients in your area if they give you, say, 5% of resulting sales in-kind. It's not difficult to find customers, as people are desperate for quality home-delivered mulch. By having the mulch delivered to your front nature strip, you'll find eager types gathering around to ask for the name of your supplier. Sign them up.

Sometimes your mulch supplier may sell cheap spoilt hay — hay that's wet and turning mouldy. Expect a good discount as it's heavy and hard work and they're desperate to offload it. You may want to wear a mask to cover your mouth and nose while putting it out to avoid breathing in spores.

To make your own mulch from garden prunings buy an electric or petrol mulcher, or split the cost with a neighbour or friend. This is better than throwing prunings away but be aware that it is harder work than it looks, and you may be disappointed after a hard mornings work to find a relatively small pile of mulch.

Do It Yourself

Attractive plants, such as this daylily, can be divided easily and distributed throughout the garden.

When your garden is in its early stages, search the neighbourhood for food growing on trees — there's often a fair bit around. We harvest macadamias, small-leaved lilly pillies, native tamarind and sandpaper figs from public areas. Make sure it's not growing alongside major roadways as it could be polluted.

If self-sown seeds are sprouting in your garden and you want to keep them, either let them grow where they are or spread them around. (Ensure they are not potential weeds.)

Rather than raising seeds and cuttings just for yourself, grow extra so you can swap them with other people for species you don't have.

Arrange to propagate other people's seeds and come to an arrangement over what materials they supply. In return you could get a negotiated percentage of the seedlings.

Walk around friends' gardens with secateurs in hand. Have plastic bags for the cuttings.

Often there are ways to turn annuals into perennials or at least to extend their lifetimes. For example: keep on harvesting the reshooting heads of your broccoli (the marketers have now caught on and sell these as cute broccolini — without such a cute price); cut just above the base of the spring onions so they reshoot; and grow open-hearted lettuce you can continually pluck from the outside. Keep the nutrients up to these constant providers.

Garden Wise

Do you find your garden is an avenue through which you can express yourself? Or is it a never-ending list of tasks that need doing? Are you still hoping a TV gardening show will select your place for an overnight makeover? Gardening can be a creative joy, not just a constant response to problems. Most garden difficulties can be designed away, but for those problems that sneak through the design web, this chapter shows how to nip them in the bud.

Daylily flowers and buds are tasty sautéed with a touch of cream and pepper.

O ne way to make the work a pleasure is to focus on what has been done, not the work ahead. Start close to the house with speedily achievable projects that create a feature, such as an entranceway, a small herb spiral or a pond.

There could be no other occupation like gardening in which, if you were to creep up behind someone at their work, you would find them smiling.
Mirabel Osler A Gentle Plea For Chaos

Watch out — there's only one week between a zucchini and a marrow.

It helps if they're visual and functional so you can continually see the work you've done. Maybe it could be something that involves friends and can be used early on — like a barbecue area. Invite friends for a feast and perhaps ask them to bring an interesting plant to be grown around the barbecue area and eventually be used in cooking, such as rosemary or a lemon tree. They may want to help plant it and, with the thought of tasting it in the years to come, they could have a greater interest in the garden.

This improved garden area can then be a central place to work out from. It's easier to maintain sections and create a greater impact when areas adjoin each other. At the same time think for the long term — what outcomes would you like that may need more time to establish, such as fruit, home-grown mulch and a living trellis to grow a passionfruit vine up? Consider planting these soon so you don't have to wait too long for your needs to be met.

Pace yourself. A spurt of enthusiasm is a good thing if it is directed into a project that is sized to match the burst, but if you go too hard too fast and hope to complete the grand plan in a single go you may find none of the projects get finished. Nature revels in chaos and will soon fill uncompleted spaces with her own ideas.

Australia's blue-banded bee is worth nurturing; it pollinates well without the sting.

Get Other People Involved for Free

My initial foray into gardening was as a WWOOFER, a Willing Worker On Organic Farms. This entailed working on farms or gardens (that aren't necessarily fully organic) for around four hours a day in return for board and food. I met great people, learnt a lot and I trust they got good work out of me.

Once I was spot mulching so many trees that when I finally straightened up and looked back, I realised I'd even mulched around the base of a power-pole. It was time for a break.

Gardening activities that seem laborious for one person may be a delight for another — especially if they haven't done it before. Hosting WWOOFERS can be a positive experience for yourself and the garden. If you don't have a lot of time or energy to interact with them, look for a couple — they'll be able to amuse each other without you.

It helps if WWOOFERS are recommended by someone else. You may want to casually interview them on the phone first. Often, it's easier if they come for longer periods so they can understand the garden, as well as the household dynamics.

Sharing a task doubles the fun.

One dynamo WWOOFER worked with us for three months. She'd completed both a Landscaping and Permaculture Design Course and she helped transform the garden. She taught me a lot and nurtured special parts of the garden — although, since she left, I've never been able to make the pot plants look quite so healthy.

Like many things in life, you're bound to find 'willing' helpers if there's something in it for them. This doesn't have to be a financial reward: many people will be pleased to help out in return for some of the harvest. Older people or immigrants, who may once have had a splendid garden but might not have the room or energy any more, may gladly help out in return for some juicy tomatoes or just to get their hands dirty again.

Another way to enlist the help of fellow gardeners is to start an informal gardening group. With a small party of friends working on each other's gardens on a rotational basis, you will be able to give each garden a facelift and each gardener an uplift.

If you can't find people to share-garden with, then maybe teach someone how to garden in exchange for their lending a hand. Give them interesting tasks so they can learn. Conversely, you could swap other skills for a bit of garden support: if you're a hairdresser, why not give a family a haircut and you've got a whole spruced-up team to help out.

Kids have a natural affinity for being outdoors and what they find often surprises them — when they discover, for example, that a pineapple doesn't actually hang from a tree, but is a bromeliad growing on the ground. Another surprise is the pineapple's spiky top, which can simply be cut off, the base cleaned back, left in the shade for a few days and then replanted to grow again. Many kids enjoy gardening when it has an element of risk and power — like boys using machetes. So train them well, ensure they're dressed appropriately and keep an eye on them. Only allow them to do it for short periods so they don't lose concentration and a leg. Easy jobs for the machete include cutting banana suckers, arrowroot, weeds and other fleshy plants.

When kids demand extra pocket money give them a clearly defined gardening goal. Gardening especially helps kids with low self-esteem and those needing exercise.

Childhood delight of harvesting and preparing food.

Planting, Feeding and Watering Fruit Trees

ike preparing a baby's nursery before its birth, it helps to make a fruit tree's bed long before it arrives. If possible, figure out where they're going to be, prepare the soil with fertilisers and organic matter, and mulch out the grass. Use a variety of different-sized mulches to attract different soil organisms. The fruit trees will love their new home and settle in quickly.

If you nurture fruit and nut trees when they're young, such as this pecan, they'll nurture you into retirement.

If you're planning a large orchard you can make a big difference by pre-working the ground. Deep-rip the soil with either a chisel plough, a Yeoman's plough or the Wallace Soil Reconditioner. These all reach under the soil, lifting it and breaking it without turning it over. Deep-rip either along the contour to catch water run-off, or slightly off contour to direct more water to drier ridges. Do this at least two months before planting the fruit trees and grow a green manure crop. Then slash the crop back before flowering to release its nitrogen into the soil. Plant the fruit trees. They will be healthy if their roots can expand easily, and they won't be shocked from contact with fresh fertiliser.

Kindergarten kids aren't primed to tough it out in the big wide world and it's the same with a young tree from the nursery. Sometimes it has been pampered to seduce buyers and may not be a weather warrior. So, after buying a tree, it may need to be slowly acclimatised to the sun, wind or cold for a week or two. If possible, it's better to buy ones that have been grown outside and exposed to the weather so you can witness what conditions they'll not only endure, but thrive in.

Plant fruit trees out when conditions aren't extreme. Overcast and still days are best — when there's little chance of hot sun, wind or frost. If necessary, give them protection against unpredictable weather. Dig a hole at least twice as big as the pot so their roots can stretch out, rather than remain root bound. If the soil is clay-based, don't make sharp edges on the hole with a spade; break up the walls or a little dam may be created even after the tree is planted and the soil put back in. Massage the rest of the soil and soften it up. Mix in a little fertiliser and organic matter but not so much that there are air pockets.

Before planting the tree water it in its pot so it is less shocked when its roots are disturbed. If it's really root bound then tease the roots out a bit, but gently. If the soil starts to break away from the roots try to hold it in as much as possible.

When the plant is lowered into the soil and standing straight its potting mix should be about the same level as the ground. Lightly push down the soil around it to get rid of any large air pockets. Check again to see it's standing straight. If it could be lost in long grass or weeds, stake it, preferably on its uphill side to stop mulch sliding onto it. Be careful not to drive the stake through its major roots. Unless it's really windy and can't stand up on its own, don't tie it to the stake — it's better for it to create its own woody tissue in its stem to counteract the wind.

Put fertiliser around it — more on the uphill side as it will gradually leach downhill. This also encourages the growth of uphill roots that are vital for wind resistance. Water well. Mulch about a 1-metre diameter with cardboard or newspaper and then hay, making sure it comes close to the plant's stem to keep out weeds, but doesn't touch it and cause stem rot.

Cut back on its water as it establishes itself. It may be accustomed to two waters per day in the nursery — cut it down to a single and then even less as you see fit.

Tougher trees such as mulberries are a boon to time-strapped or inexperienced gardeners.

Pest-reducing Strategies

A long time ago, I had a boyfriend whose mother meticulously tied pink bows around the few bean plants to survive a pest infestation. She wanted to keep their non-hybrid seeds and disseminate their naturally evolved genes so that she wouldn't have to revert to chemicals to control the pests. How was I to know? She was out one day when I strolled down the garden. The bright ribbons caught my eye drawing me to the healthiest and tastiest looking beans. I hoed in. Perhaps that's why he's a former boyfriend.

Bagging fruit, not people, is a relaxing form of active meditation. A neighbour, who is tantalised each day as she walks past, has just asked me if she can help bag the fruit-fly prone feijoas. She has an ulterior motive.

It's a clever strategy; keeping only those plants that display strong genes and are pest resistant will ensure future crops retain these characteristics. Ensure they are grown from non-hybrid seed as they produce off-spring that is true to type. Also cull for strong genes. If growing seedlings, for example, pot up the healthiest half only. Then only plant out the healthiest half of these. When they seed, save the seeds from the plants that demonstrate the most pest-resistant characteristics for growing next season.

Another strategy to minimise the damage from pests is to keep the soil fertile, with plenty of micro-nutrients. That way the plants have the strength to fight diseases and recover from pest damage. If your plants are suffering, spray their leaves with seaweed fertiliser — this is a good all-round fertiliser that will help them build up their resistance. In the long

Before acting, observe pests and how much damage they really do. This katydid looks ravenous but only nibbles parts of plants we don't eat. Some species actually eat pests.

term, this is far more helpful than spraying poisons. Before reaching for any pesticide, try growing plants that attract pest predators. These are detailed in the chapter called Test the Pests.

Practise crop rotation — avoid planting the same families after each other so there is less chance of pests continuing to thrive. After a heavy feeding crop, such as broccoli, plant a legume to put nitrogen back into the soil.

Often so-called pests may look ravenous and dangerous but inflict little harm in the garden. Only use sprays as a last option. Even organic pesticides that sound innocent may kill beneficial predators as well.

Weed-reducing Strategies

Watch out for people coated with weed seeds. Sometimes when I have groups visiting, they have just come from a property that has sticky weed seeds. I know because they arrive decorated with them. I figure my talk is becoming boring when I see them plucking the seeds off their pants. While I explain the intricacies of weed management, they toss noxious weed seeds into our garden. These days I begin with a word of caution. Pluck weed seeds off while inside the house — not in the garden. Throw them in the bin, not the compost (where some can survive and thrive posthumusly).

Eliminate the worst weeds in the garden as soon as possible, preferably before they seed. Most running weeds can be killed by being pulled out and piled up in a hot, sunny area with black plastic over them. Burn any really rampant weeds or take them to the tip.

Use pulled-up weeds as mulch only if they won't spread. If they've already gone to seed and you desperately want to use them, then use them in an ecology they are not suited to. For example, use sun-loving weeds to mulch shady areas. Less-noxious weeds without seeds are unlikely to flourish if they're placed on top of cardboard.

A weed mat woven by nature — multi-layered shading.

One of our many edible herbicides — zucchinis —
out-compete weeds and are a garden staple.

Just a moment of sunlight can trigger some weed seeds to sprout, so try not to expose bare patches of soil to sunlight. Plant under-utilised areas in waiting with cover crops or green manure crops.

Water entices weeds, so keep it away from pathways and only irrigate plants when and where necessary.

Combined with good design, all of these ideas help keep weeds down, avoiding or reducing the need to spray poisons. I do everything possible to avoid poisons, although I have resorted to them on three occasions to help turn a weed forest into a native rainforest. In each of these cases we painted the stumps of

privet to stop them suckering. We did this within a few seconds of the trees being cut so that the stumps sucked in the mixture before they sealed off.

Alongside this we are doing trials without poison to see how long the stumps will continue to regrow if we continually cut back the suckers, giving less time for photosynthesis to occur. After four years quite a few stumps have died out, some are petering out and others are still resprouting.

Using Less Water

Before the hot weather arrives, let the trees grow to create more shade. Later they can be pruned to let the winter sun in. Although, if frost is likely to be a problem, don't open up the garden too much.

A water-efficient garden can grow striking plants like roses, not just cacti.

The best way to protect the soil from hot sun and drying wind is to use mulch. When you do water, do so heavily and less often so plants are encouraged to send their roots out and down. Water on the uphill side of plants so that the water slowly filters into the root systems, rather than escaping downhill.

Monitor the moist and dry areas of the garden and plant and water accordingly. Observe and maintain any water strategies that you may have in place, such as swales and diversion drains. Check to see they are spreading the water over a wide area and it is not converging.

Rather than giving all fruit trees the same amount of water, try to understand their particular water requirements and at what stage of their production cycle they may need less or more. Good fruit tree books help.

Working with Frost

You'll know when it's frosty, as it's the most difficult time to get out of bed. It helps to have the thermal underwear and woollen clothes ready by the bed, so they can be slipped on under the doona. The boots may be a different story.

Taste the changing seasons, they offer the opportunity to grow different vegetables. The first crunch of snow peas brings a winter garden to life.

On frosty mornings before the sun rises, turn on the vegie garden sprinkler. This helps thaw the plants, reducing the damage caused by sun hitting frozen cells — often causing them to burst.

You can prevent frost settling by retaining excess foliage in winter — even if it looks cold-affected and straggly. In areas with a slope, allow grass to grow quite high around susceptible plants, especially if there's no great pressure to keep it tidy. Mulch and stake trees well so they're not lost.

If possible, cut the most elevated section of this grass slightly off contour so it diverts the frost downhill, away from the tender plants. If not possible, be aware frost could bank up behind the grass and affect other vulnerable plants in this area. If necessary protect them with frost barriers (see page 112) or cover them with a heat-retaining plastic woven cloth.

Add potash to the soil in autumn to harden new growth. Don't encourage too much new growth in autumn and winter — reduce fertiliser, water and singing. Don't plant the spring crop too early.

Gardening to Improve Soil

When meeting someone you shake their hand. This handshake can tell you a lot about how they're feeling. When you go out into your garden, shake its hand too by picking up some soil. It's forever changing — so feel what state it's in. This helps indicate what areas to improve.

Researchers are discovering many symbiotic relationships between plants and fungi that further explain the benefits of organic growing.

There are many ways to enhance soil. If you grow multiple layers of plants, including groundcovers, the various layers of roots will break up the soil, creating channels for water and oxygen to enter, enticing soil organisms. The plants also protect the soil from the harsh sun.

Deep-rooted plants, like the daikon radish, also break up the soil, as well as mining hidden nutrients, and then when they die back they are available to other plants.

Try not to turn over the soil as it destroys the hard work the soil organisms have been doing in creating a top soil. Use a garden fork to loosen and aerate it and mix in fertiliser or make a sheet mulch garden.

Put compost, spent mushroom compost, worm castings and/or animal manure into the garden — whatever you can find. My older sister goes to the circus to collect the elephants' offerings — it's not hard to get a trailerload. (Although I sometimes wonder if they have strong deworming or other chemicals in them.) Also gather organic matter wherever you can — grass clippings, vegie scraps, newspaper, cardboard or hair.

Almost instant mulch —— simply add water, soil and inoculant to this pigeon seed mix and wait a month or so for green manure.

To boost soil nitrogen, cut the green manure crop when it is succulent and growing rapidly. Then cover it or dig it in. For bulk high-carbon mulch, cut it later.

Grow a range of annual green manure crops or perennial cover crops. These help break up the soil and may provide nitrogen. They can also keep out weeds and can be cut back and used as mulch. For more details see page 229 and page 231 respectively.

Use diverse mulch — a range of mulch types supply a range of houses for a variety of soil organisms. In return, they improve the soil and reduce the likelihood of diseases. Shrubs are a good source of mulch. The lignin in branches slowly breaks down to increase the humus in the soil. Grow shrubs that can be cut back, yet replenish quickly, such as pigeon pea and crotalaria. For longer-lasting plants use native mulberry, macaranga and many types of acacias. The acacias double up as nitrogen-fixers. When cut back, they release nitrogen into the soil. Do this at a time that suits your garden — depending on whether it needs more sunlight, refreshing breezes or when the chance of frost has gone. If you don't like the haphazard look of coarse prunings, cut them smaller or cover them with a light layer of hay mulch.

Observe Carefully

A week or two can mean the difference between a tree laden with ripening fruit and one pecked bare as Adam. With careful observation pests, such as birds, bats and possums, can prove good indicators. They often show when the first fruit is ready. This is an alarm-call to bring other fruit inside to ripen.

Contemplative observation finds unexpected harmony in everyday things, like this arrowroot leaf.

Watch out for fruit falls. On the ground they often harbour pests, such as fruit fly. These can then spread throughout the garden. Collect them as soon as possible.

Observe pest predators and how they live, and try to make them feel at home. My favourites are the comical water dragons that mainly eat insects and spiders. They love perching on warm, elevated sites, like my soil-filled boots with the cacti growing out of them. I watch them from my office. They often raise an arm as if to say hello. I want to move the boots but I think I'll leave them for the dragons.

Monitor the variation of soil moisture levels and water accordingly. Note plants affected by water stress — and act before major damage occurs. Be especially mindful of fruit trees as they can take longer to show serious stress. By the time they do manifest symptoms it could be a case of long-term damage or worse.

We had a Davidson's plum and star apple that both started to show signs of water stress. I didn't take their signs seriously enough and then no matter how I watered them they died.

Do Things for the Long Term

*I*f something is done half-heartedly, it feels like a task. If it's done well it's enjoyable.

I used to be parsimonious, and paid the price. For example, I made a passionfruit trellis out of fishing-pole bamboo. In one year the trellis collapsed, yet the plant persisted for four years, in a scrambled mess.

It's great to use natural materials where appropriate, like bamboo stakes for short-term crops such as tomatoes, but for the longer term it pays to think ahead. Our garden arch is made to last. It has four star-pickets with polypipe hooping over the top and plastic mesh in between for plants to climb. It's solid and dependable and should last a good 20 years.

It's also important to make pathways well as they're such an integral part of the garden. The same with buying tools: shoddy secateurs crush branch edges, increasing the chance of diseases; a cheap mattock gives splinters and its top can fly off, like a weapon in a James Bond movie.

Long winter nights are good opportunities to plan, research and gather inspiration for the next phase of the garden.

Gardening Tidbits

ere are a few hints that I've taken on board from other people or discovered for myself. Tick the ones you could use:

- Begin gardening by stomping on your gloves to squish any overnighting bities.

- Discretely stake or put solid rocks on the corners of the garden that the hose is pulled around — this stops it flattening plants.

Rock features on garden corners protect delicate flowers from being crushed by hoses taking shortcuts.

- One of the most challenging tasks that often needs doing early on is earthmoving. To ease anxieties, you may want a consultant to help you discuss any earthworks you envisage, as well as advising the driver on your behalf. Peg out what it is you want together and before the earthmover arrives. Machines can seem ominous at first but, by watching carefully, you may see how they work with the choreographic skills of ballet dancers. But don't take the consultant away for a cup of tea while the machine's working. It may have moved the earth for you — but offloaded it right where you want the sunken garden amphitheatre.

- Don't necessarily select an earthmover because it is available immediately. Plan ahead and patiently choose quality: someone who has many satisfied clients and a steady track record.

Grow runaway plants, such as mint and stinging nettles, in pots. Rampant plants can be wonderful at first — we thrive on their productivity — but secretly they harbour plans for world domination. Through careful management we can benefit from their ambition. Move the pots around so the plants don't root into the soil, and prune any plants before they seed. (Some tribes in Papua New Guinea hit women with stinging nettle while they're giving birth. Apparently they don't feel the birth pain so much. Some Australians whip themselves with it to reduce the effects of arthritis. We're not quite so brave. We eat it like spinach, mainly for its high iron content. It's important to cook it first, otherwise you'll momentarily forget any problem you ever had.)

Kid's gardening instincts can be nurtured by letting them choose a fun outdoor ornament and a special place to put it.

Create Tool Collection Points throughout the garden. Drop tools at the designated points while gardening and save time by not searching for those secateurs.

Have a drinking water tap outside — so you and other workers don't have to tramp through the house to replenish. You're less likely to dehydrate.

Don't answer the phone — leave the answering machine on and enjoy time out. It's so disrupting to rush inside with muddy boots and hands only to be hounded by a carpet-cleaning salesperson — although, you may find they are now needed.

Lie in the garden for a break — see things from a beetle's perspective. Watch the clouds.

Mark the water main. It's rarely thought about, but when it's needed it's usually an emergency — people accidentally dig through a pipe and the water gushes up like a geyser. Inform house-sitters as well.

Document not only the species, but the varieties of fruit trees. (Their tags inevitably fall off.) I can remember the species of our 120 fruit trees, but not their varieties. So we document them as we plant them. This helps us learn which varieties fruit best in our conditions, which ones are most pest resistant and what conditions they prefer.

The practice of foot binding is now outlawed. Plants also suffer from forgotten ties.

Make a pruning diary to remember trees that need pruning at different times of the year.

Be clear before the chainsaw comes out. I looked out the window while I was writing this book to see some acacias falling. Dean and I had discussed the trees to cut earlier, however the discussion was casual and undecided. Chainsaws and ambiguity are a dangerous couple.

Take time just to wander through the garden at different times of day and learn from all the interactions you see. Wise pondering saves a lot of hard work in the long term.

Rats imagine there are delicious seeds inside drip irrigation and chew through it. Whipper snippers have a mind of their own and also do damage. Sections of pipe protect the drippers.

Prepare for the whipper snipper — stake and mulch seedlings so they are readily identifiable, and won't be ringbarked by the cord. This kills them.

A creaky gate alerts you to visitors so they don't sneak up on you unexpectedly.

Prepare the garden before hard structures are put in. After we put down our sandstone paving we realised we wanted to run irrigation lines to the kiwifruit and grapevine. It was too late.

Protect drip irrigation.

Gardening late into winter afternoons stretches the short days.

The purple glow of the full moon can transform a garden — finding edges in patterned foliage. Plant some drama for moonlit walks.

Water weeds can be the worst: get on top of them first. Spreading faster than most land weeds, water weeds are difficult to eliminate and can have detrimental effects. Once our dam was covered so thickly by a native water weed, azolla, that a visitor mistook the dam for a concrete skateboard rink. The silver perch were gasping for air and sadly asphyxiated. A bit too late, we decided we needed to interfere. Using two surfboards and a long strip of shade cloth we mustered the weed like cattle. Being high in nitrogen, we mulched it on the citrus. Now we keep on top of the azolla as soon as we see it returning although it rarely begins to take off as we have a more balanced ecology.

A timer for the main watering tap. My brother wishes he used one. He took his first handyman job in the luxurious garden surrounds of an elite block of apartments. He made a common workman's mistake — turning on the sprinklers and then going home to play cards. It was an enthralling game, sadly disrupted hours later when a resident called to say some of the garden was floating down the main road. It's easy to prevent this occurring. With a mere twist of the dial a simple timer ensures the garden is watered appropriately. The outlay is soon recouped — lower water bills, no flooded gardens and most importantly, an uninterrupted game of cards.

Affordable and Effective Practical Projects

This chapter highlights some of the important features

of a permaculture garden; the cogs that turn it around

so that it can power ahead. It includes a guide to

making: a herb spiral; an attractive pond; a lasagne

garden; a worm farm, a cover crop and a home brew

(for the plants, not you). Also learn how to make a

weedy area more productive and build an effective

'Swale of the Century'.

A dragonfly on a native waterlily.

Much Ado About Mulching

From the Queen of Mulchavia

Most people have at least one outstanding skill, whether it be juggling, negotiating peace or hitchhiking across Ireland with a fridge. Mine is mulching.

It is my opinion that this talent hasn't been given the accolades, let alone the recognition, it deserves. So I'm putting it on a pedestal and using up my 15 minutes of fame.

Suffering from kikuyu-grass blues, I designed to overcome lawn and order. To checkmate this speedy invader, I used the strategies of chess — blocking defensively and not leaving any weak edge for invasion.

I did leave some grass, however. I actually like it in a useful area, just not too much. Grass can be hard work and often takes the potential place of fruitful plants. Not only is it highly competitive, it is often allelopathic, that is, it exudes a chemical that retards the growth of

It helps if you can get flattened cardboard in bulk bales. This comes from the supermarket via our local Wastebusters and costs only $5.

Borage self-seeds readily and can grow up through thick mulch. It adds a beautiful spark of blue to the garden and when it is dying off it can be cut back to add another mulch layer.

neighbouring species. This is a common cause of stunted growth and paleness in plants, especially shallow-rooted trees such as citrus.

I overcame the main problems of weeds and grass in the early design phases, and since then have been trying to garden with forethought. One of the most effective things I did, with long-term results, was sheet mulching. The beauty of mulching is you don't have to pull out the weeds, and it is also appropriate for converting larger areas. It uses overlapping layers of newspaper or cardboard and hay to smother weeds. Over time, as the plants, roots and mulch layers decompose, the underlying soil gets a boost.

Before I bought this house and land it had been the festivity magnet of the area, with visitors galore — and their cars. As we're quiet types we transformed one of the compacted car-parking sections into edible groundcovers and hardy fruit trees.

We started by planting into the grassy areas and sheet mulched over every bit of land around the plants. Within three months not a blade of grass was left and it was establishing dinosaur gourds, water-melons, sweet potatoes, a white sapote, bananas and an ice-cream bean tree. It is a formula we've kept to and is still helping to transform the place.

In areas that are heavily mulched to get rid of weeds, grow pioneer crops such as corn, watermelon and pumpkin. They can tolerate mulch around their stems and quickly form a living mulch, which eventually adds to what is already there.

How to Sheet Mulch

You will need the following materials:
Newspaper/cardboard; mulch (hay/pea straw/lucerne); plants; fertiliser; stakes; water.

1 If necessary, trample or slash the grass or weeds.

2 Strategically place out the trees, bushes and groundcovers you want to plant. Dig the prospective holes, add organic fertiliser and plant.

3 Place stakes uphill of the plants and close by. This helps prevent the cardboard/newspaper and mulch slipping onto them causing their stems to rot. It has the additional advantage of allowing you to find the plants in the fluffy mulch. Bamboo stakes are relatively cheap — double their value by cutting them in half; they only need to be just higher than the mulch.

4 For every square metre of grass or weeds, throw down a handful of nitrogen fertiliser, such as chook manure, pellets or blood and bone. The bacteria in the soil will use this nitrogen to balance their diet when they're eating the high-carbon cardboard/newspaper. If this extra nitrogen is not supplied they'll take it from the soil, and hence the plants.

5 Water the area well.

6 Cover the area with overlapping layers of double cardboard or, if you are using newspaper, lay it ten sheets thick. To prevent weeds raising their heads at the first opportunity, cover any gaps in the cardboard. Ensure materials are laid close to the plants but don't let them touch.

7 Spread the mulch on top, 15-centimetres thick if you can afford it. You can get away with using less mulch, however, if you use the number of layers of newspaper or cardboard suggested. In low-rainfall areas, use less mulch as it reduces the amount of water seeping through.

With really compacted soil and/or thick weeds it may be initially too difficult to dig a hole. And in those areas where you need to grow plants really closely, such as in the herb and vegetable garden, it can become tricky laying cardboard around them. In both these cases, mulch the whole area. Allow the grass/weeds/cardboard/newspaper a few months to start decomposing and then break open the cardboard and plant directly into the soil. The decomposed roots of the grass/weeds and the cardboard will be a lot more forgiving.

Whenever I hand-water a mulched area I put the hose under the mulch so less water evaporates from the hay.

Lasagne Gardening

Shock your partner! While they're away start a vegetable garden on the weed patch or that useless bit of concrete out the back. There is a brilliant technique for doing just this — without the sweat and toil of breaking up the surface. It's called No-dig Gardening and it was developed by the Australian gardener, Esther Dean who, following an illness, found herself unable to dig heavy soil but was determined to keep gardening. The technique involves spreading lots of different materials — layer by layer — just like lasagne.

This type of gardening is so appealing because it smothers weeds — no pulling needed. It helps if it's placed where few of its edges back onto grass or weeds as they can raid the rich garden in the long term.

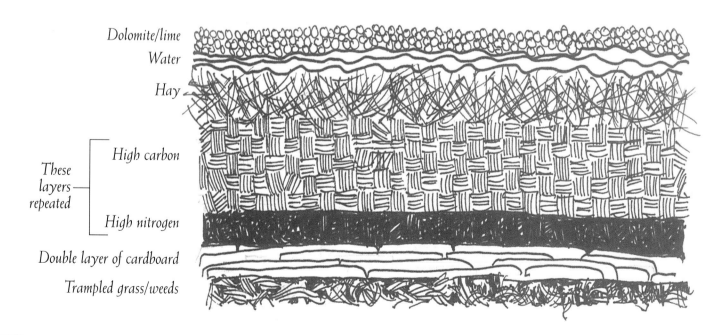

Dolomite/lime
Water
Hay

High carbon

These layers repeated

High nitrogen

Double layer of cardboard
Trampled grass/weeds

How to Make a No-dig Garden

No-dig vegie gardens initially gobble up materials so begin with a small area. Then expand as you appreciate how simple it is…converting concrete jungles into gardens of Eden.

The lasagne feast will end up being about 80 centimetres high. There may be up to 10 times as much carbon materials as there are nitrogen materials, as the former is much bulkier. However, the nitrogen is still essential.

The lasagne garden has many of the benefits of a big compost heap — yet its smaller nitrogen to carbon ratio means it is not so hot and so will not burn seedlings.

You will need the following materials:

10 parts high-carbon materials: such as hay, dead leaves, newspaper or cardboard (it helps to take any sticky tape off), sawdust, old grass clippings, the family's fingernail clippings.

1 part high-nitrogen materials: such as manure/fertiliser pellets, vegie scraps, green leaves, stems or grass, hair, blood and bone (fertiliser).

Other ingredients: lime/dolomite, water, old cotton sheet (not vital), some garden soil, seedlings.

1. Select a patch of grass, weeds or concrete near the house. Trample it. Don't bother if it's concrete, unless you're trying to get fit.

2. For the grassy/weedy areas throw on some of the high-nitrogen materials. These help to break down the grass and weeds and to attract the neighbours' lawn-avoiding worms.

3. Put down a double layer of cardboard, overlapping it well. Ten layers of newspaper can be used instead. This is all the newspaper/cardboard that will be used.

4. Now alternate layers of high-nitrogen with layers of high-carbon materials until it's over 80 centimetres high. The carbon layers will be about 10 times as thick as the nitrogen. Water as you go. Like a lasagne, the richer the ingredients, the tastier the end result.

5. The last layer is hay.

6. Sprinkle with dolomite/lime and water well.

7. If you want fast food you can plant into it straight away. To do this, make holes and pour into them half a bucket of garden soil and plant the vegie seedlings in it. Don't consider root crops, such as carrots, until the second year.

8. You won't need as much soil for the holes if you let it break down for about eight weeks. Cover it with hessian or an old sheet to reduce water loss and encourage decomposition. Then plant it out.

Composing Pathways

Pathways and accesses can make or break a garden, so it's worth establishing them early. Be aware, however, that the placement of pathways may change, so if you're unsure don't start by constructing permanent ones.

Paths made of bark or similar natural materials can display fallen petals without needing to be swept or blown.

We experimented with a number of path-building materials. The sawdust was good value as it was free from the timber mill, but it wasn't so attractive when it walked into the house. It also broke down too quickly and in heavy rains riverlets gouged through steep areas. We ended up shovelling it onto the vegie garden.

Next, we tried pebbles. These, however, felt uncomfortable to walk on in bare feet and shifted underfoot. We finally settled on soft, small bark chips.

Bark pathways last for a long time if they're about 10 centimetres thick. If you're converting grass or weeds into pathway then put double cardboard or long-lasting weed mat from the nursery under the bark. This prevents the grass and weeds leaping through it. Although weed mat is far more expensive, it is better to use it on a slope as the cardboard can slide underfoot, giving you an unexpected tobogganing experience.

Bark is an easy material to distribute. Pile more in the centre of the paths, as feet naturally spread it, and more on the uphill sections, as it finds its way downhill. Further away from the house the path can become narrower where it is less frequently used. This also tricks the eye into believing the garden is longer.

Build a Herb Spiral

Herb spirals are great for a number of reasons. Instead of buying a bigger block of land you can just create space by expanding upwards, not outwards. This also creates different micro-climates, ranging from shady moist areas to warmer drier areas.

Herb spirals are also terrific in wet areas as they create well-drained places, especially at the top. Conversely, in dry areas the plants down the bottom of the spiral thrive on the extra moisture.

Heat-loving plants face north and west

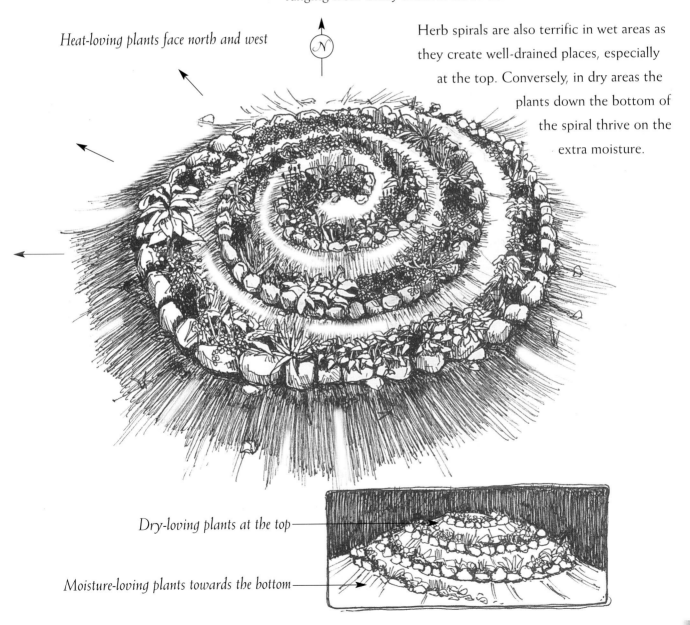

Dry-loving plants at the top

Moisture-loving plants towards the bottom

You will need the following materials:
Soil; rocks; seedlings; mulch; water.

1 Start with a mound of soil the size you want the spiral to eventually be. Ensure the most fertile soil is on the outside layer. If you have any old rubble you want to get rid of, you can reinforce the middle of the mound with this, then place a generous amount of soil over it. This works well when you need to improve drainage.

2 Place the largest rocks around the bottom of the mound — spiralling them up to the top as they get smaller, yet leaving a lot of the soil uncovered. Try to make all parts of the spiral readily accessible. In areas that aren't, grow plants that don't need a lot of attention, such as flowers.

3 Mulch, plant and water well.

Yarrow attracts wildlife; its leaves added to compost speed up decomposition and its cut flowers dry beautifully for display.

Herbs That Prefer Moist Conditions
(plant near the bottom of the spiral — facing the softer morning sun)

Bergamot	Lemon balm
Borage	Mint (in a pot)
Coriander	Mushroom plant
Cress	Parsley
French tarragon	Rocket
Ginger	Vietnamese mint (in a pot)
Lebanese cress (in a pot)	Watercress

Herbs That Prefer/ Handle Drier Conditions
(plant facing the summer sun and on top of the spiral)

Garlic chives	Rosemary
Lavender	Yarrow
Marjoram	Society garlic
Oregano	Thyme

Make a Pond

Just a little permanent water in the garden can attract pest predators, create beneficial micro-climates and cultivate relaxing thoughts. Make sure it is not a potential danger for young children.

Dragonflies simply devour mosquito problems.

You will need the following materials:

Newspaper; pool lining/butyl rubber (lasts up to 20 years); rocks; water; frog log; aquatic plants (in pots if necessary).

1 If possible, select a relatively flat piece of land so soil edges don't jut out of the water on the uphill side, like the white cliffs of Dover. An area that catches water run-off will need less refilling.

2 Dig a hole the size you want your pond to be. Don't make it smooth-sided — leave

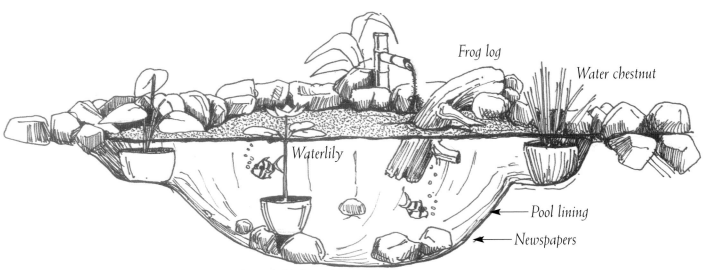

Frog log

Water chestnut

Waterlily

Pool lining

Newspapers

Rocks to hold down lining

some ledges in it for submerged pot plants. If you want, create a slightly lower area on one edge so that a bit of water can seep into the nearby soil, creating a perfect place for semi-aquatic plants such as kangkong. In North Vietnam we ate this in a lot of dishes, stir-fried with garlic, ginger and tofu. It's an annual in cooler areas, a perennial where it's warmer. Within weeks it will start to float on the water and not long after the leaves and crunchy stems can begin to be harvested. Keep an eye on this plant, making sure it doesn't become too free-living and smother the pond.

3 Cover the dug-out area and garden edges with overlapping newspaper — 10 layers thick. Then cover the newspaper with pool lining or butyl rubber.

4 Carefully put some rocks down the bottom to anchor the lining. Display the most beautiful rocks around the edge and slightly hanging over the top of the pond so they are most visible. They also help to hide the lining and reduce the amount of sun hitting it.

5 Fill with water.

6 Immerse in the pond large, soil-filled pots with aquatic plants in them, such as lotus, taro and water lilies.

7 Put in a frog log so animals can use it to get out of the water. Otherwise the pond could become a large brew of frog-leg soup.

Invite some great barred frogs over for a risqué pool party — you'll be surprised what they get up to over a few drinks after cracking a bit of chitin — grasshopper legs preferred.

Make Your Own Worm Farm

*I*f we were able to have entered biblical Eden, the first thing to arouse our senses might have been the fresh smell of humus. Good gardening is not so much about cultivating plants, but cultivating the soil. Here are some techniques:

One inventive South Australian has a big metal box to sit on for outside meals, complete with an in-built cushion. But that isn't all. His meal over, he stands up, lifts the lid and throws in all his food scraps. There is a worm farm sealed within.

Many ready-made worm farms are expensive. Some are worth it, as they're designed to save time by naturally sorting the castings from the worms. However, a homemade one can be constructed more cost-effectively and designed to sort the castings also. Managing a worm farm is a great job for kids as they yield to their fascination for the earthy. They get their kind of fun, you get the black gold.

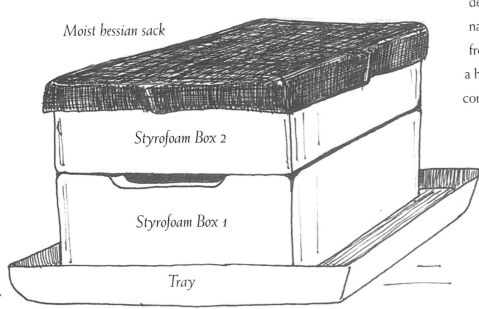

Moist hessian sack

Styrofoam Box 2

Styrofoam Box 1

Tray

You will need the following materials:

Two same-sized Styrofoam boxes: (about 60 x 40 centimetres) with about 20 small holes made in each base for any excess water to drain. These holes should be slightly bigger than a worm, but not by much. No lids are necessary. Try your greengrocer or local restaurants and supermarkets.

A large tray to put the bottom box on.

Soil/peat to fill half of one box.

Small food scraps (not oranges or onions).

Lime.

Hessian sack.

1000 manurial worms: these are available from commercial and other worm farms and are generally not the larger ones used for fish bait. Don't try to save money by cutting 500 in half. Fastidiously picking 1000 out of the garden doesn't work either — these ones are likely to be earthmovers and shakers and wouldn't survive.

1 In a shady area, put all the worms into Box 1 with the soil/peat. Keep it moist but not wet; it should feel like a damp sponge that has been squeezed, with no water coming out. (If the worm farm gets too dry, sprinkle a bit of water on one half. By only sprinkling over half the area the worms can escape to the other half if they're shocked, and then readjust slowly.)

Put the box on the tray so the worms are less likely to escape. Put a moist hessian sack on top to keep the worms in.

2 Feed them with food scraps on the first day and then as needed (they eat their body weight in food each day).

3 Continue to feed the worms until Box 1 is full (right to the top) and all the food scraps have been converted to black worm castings — small round black sausages that are more distinctly globular than soil particles.

4 Take off the hessian and put Box 2 on top. Put delicious food scraps into it and over time the socially aspiring poop masters will worm their way up through the holes in Box 1 to the new penthouse suite. This is an easy way of sorting the worms from their castings.

5 When Box 2 is also full, spread the wormless castings in Box 1 into a lush, moist part of the garden. Although there will be few worms there will be lots of worm eggs. If conditions are beneficial the eggs will hatch and gradually move around the more appealing parts of the garden. (Any remaining worms may suffer more from shock and not survive.)

6 Put Box 1, now empty, on top of Box 2, which is still full of worms. Then continue the process by putting food into the new top box. Always cover the top box with the hessian.

7 If the worm farm becomes too acidic, tiny white worms will wriggle around. These are scuttlefly larvae, not baby earthworms, and they indicate that you need to sprinkle lime over half the area.

Make a Compost Heap

I don't make compost heaps per se as our property is designed to compost on its own while I'm inside drinking tea. All our food scraps go into the Biolytix Filter (see page 109). It spreads composted liquid fertiliser to 30 fruit trees. We also recycle most of the plant material throughout the garden as we pull it up or cut it. If the cut branches look messy we cover them with hay. But some people like a more hands-on approach and the benefits of a great steaming compost heap are enormous. Here's how to make one.

Owl box (to get any mice)

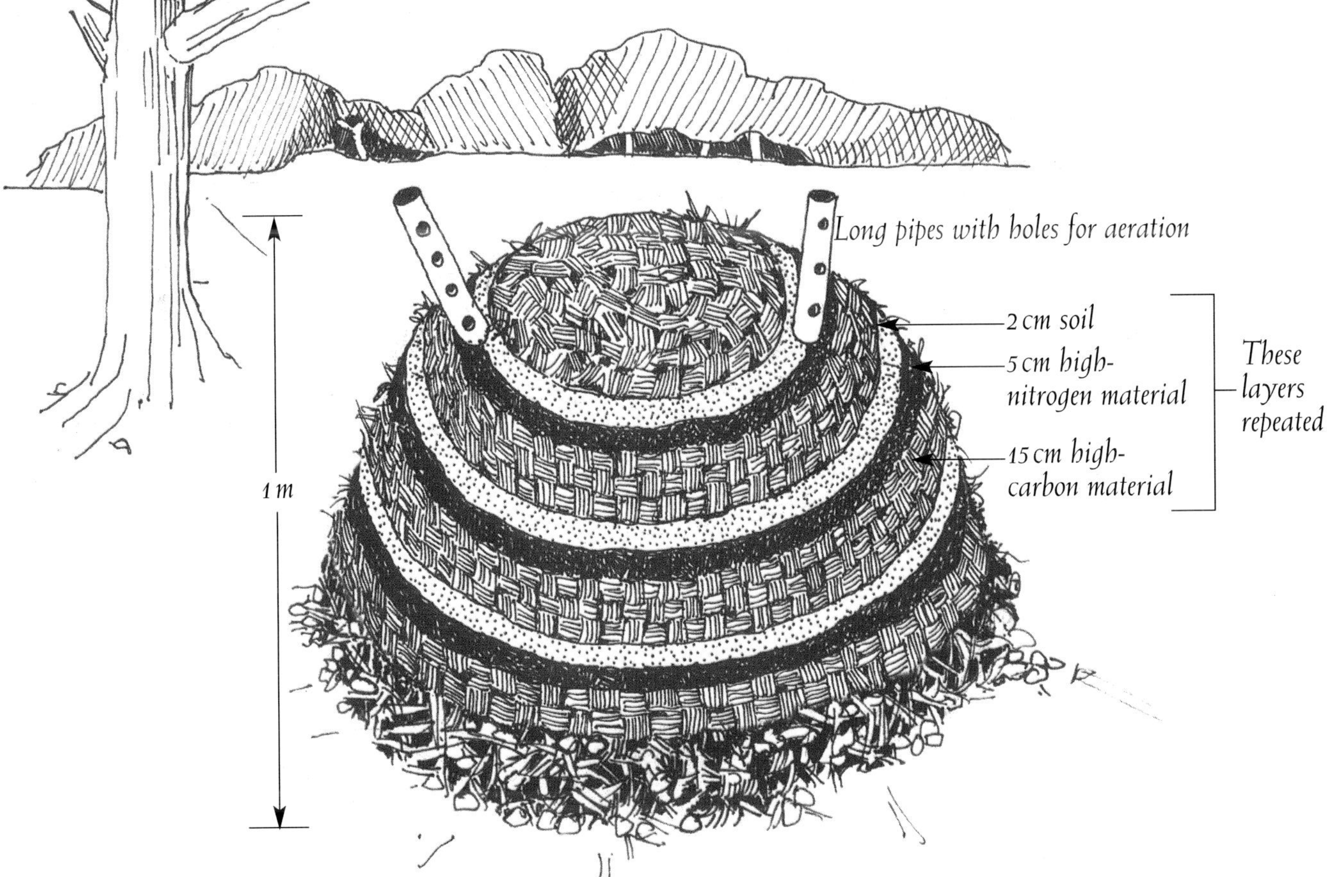

Long pipes with holes for aeration

2 cm soil

5 cm high-nitrogen material

15 cm high-carbon material

These layers repeated

1 m

1 m

Aim for a compost heap that is about one cubic metre (1 m x 1 m x 1m); sadly this will shrink. Place it uphill from an area where you could collect a wealth of run-off nutrients — like the vegie garden.

If you're worried about mice or rats place it near lateral tree branches enabling owls to perch and stalk. If this isn't feasible erect an owl box. Be careful the tree isn't so close that its roots are burnt by the compost.

You will need the following materials:
Sticks.
Plastic plumbing pipes (not vital) with holes the size of 5-cent pieces along them.
6 parts high-carbon materials (see page 217).
2 parts high-nitrogen materials (see page 217).
1 part topsoil (it helps if it has come from

another compost heap and is already teeming with microbes).
Water.

1 Put a layer of sticks on the bottom to help with aeration.

2 Stand the plumbing pipes at a slight angle in the middle of the heap-to-be to aerate it.

3 Spread a 15-centimetre layer of carbon material. Top this with 5 centimetres of nitrogen material. Then add a thin layer of topsoil. Continue layering in this way until it's 1 metre high. Water each layer.

4 After a few days it'll be perceptibly warmer. If you feel a pulse, you may even start to believe in reincarnation.

5 You don't have to turn the compost pile but it works faster if you do. Turn it on about week 2 and week 6 so the outside goes in and vice-versa. It should be ready in 10–12 weeks.

6 If you get heavy rain, or if it gets very cold, you may want to cover it with a tarpaulin.

7 Compost is a great soil conditioner — not as high in nitrogen as most fertilisers — but it adds texture and nutrients to the soil, as well as valuable micro-organisms.

Spring onions grow in most soil that is drained well but thrive if they are enriched with lots of compost.

Conjure Up a Home Brew

*I*f plants are looking a bit lacklustre or sick, give them a quick boost with homemade comfrey tea. As comfrey is deep rooted it can access a range of micro-nutrients which can be broken down to help other plants fight diseases. However, it does have a few PR problems.

Dappled shade

Shredded comfrey leaves

Home brew

One house-sitter thoughtfully added it to our pot plants to put a smile on our faces the day we returned from holidays. Instead of smiling back at the beaming plants, I scrambled frantically around the house wondering what animal had died.

Fortunately, the smell disperses in the garden a lot quicker but it can linger on the hands, so use plastic gloves to avoid splash — otherwise you might wonder why the neighbourhood dogs are following you around (although the possibility of a seat at the theatre all to yourself may be enticing).

You will need the following materials:

Rubbish bin; comfrey; water; watering can/bucket; plastic gloves; gardenia perfume

1 Fill three quarters of a big rubbish bin with comfrey leaves. Shred them to hasten decomposition.

2 Put it in dappled shade away from your bedroom window.

3 Fill with water, cover and let steep.

4 Leave for about three weeks or until the smell is no longer overpowering.

5 Dilute it 1 part liquid fertiliser:1 part water then pour it onto the soil around the plants. For pot plants dilute it 1 part liquid fertiliser: 5 parts water and put the pot outside or open the windows.

Getting Free Nitrogen from Nitrogen-fixing Plants

Nitrogen-fixing plants are amazing: they take nitrogen from the air and convert it into a rich elixir that is held in nodules along their roots. The nitrogen is released into the soil when the plants are cut back, become sick or die. Lightning is another natural way of getting nitrogen into the soil. The former is easier to generate.

By placing and pruning the plants strategically, the free fertiliser can end up where and when you want it, such as around fruit trees when they're budding. If you want to check whether particular plants are actually fixing nitrogen, examine their roots for distinct nodules. When sliced open these should be salmon pink and smell like chook pellets.

Nitrogen-fixing plants generally grow fast and take quite a bit of nitrogen from the soil in the initial process. Prune them occasionally so they release nitrogen from their roots and to ensure they don't dominate or become rampant. In arid areas, don't plant them close to fruit trees as they compete too much for water.

Some of the nitrogen-fixers, such as pigeon pea, will need to be 'mixed' or inoculated; however, many will find the *Rhizobium* bacteria they need in the soil naturally. The next section gives more details about the simple process of inoculation.

Nitrogen-fixing Trees and Shrubs

Be careful they don't become rampant in your area.

Acacias	Native pea bushes —
Albizia	pultaneas, hoveas etc
Casuarinas	Pigeon pea
Crotalaria	Siberian pea tree
Native albizia	Tagasaste
Native coral tree	Tree lupin
Native crotalaria	

Plant a Green Manure Crop

The name falls somewhat short of appetising but there's nothing unsavoury about the technique. Green manure crops are for the most part annuals (perennial crops are called Cover Crops). Many are planted because they fix nitrogen, then release it into the soil when they're cut back. Other green manure crops don't fix nitrogen but still are cut back. They may be used as a high-carbon source to improve the soil structure and fertility as well as an in-situ mulch. Each of them saves on fertiliser and has innumerable other benefits.

This crop of oats is keeping out weeds around the rainforest planting, including troublesome privet seedlings. It also helps protect the young trees from frost.

Green manure crops increase the organic matter in the soil, thereby attracting earthworms and micro-organisms. They break up compacted soil and mine deep minerals, making them more available to plants.

They smother weeds, and rapeseed, cowpea or oats help control nematodes. While you're away or feeling idle, a green manure crop is a most productive way to employ garden areas. Many species attract pest predators.

They are easy to grow and can be used readily. They're especially good after the soil is exposed from earthworks and vulnerable to erosion and weed infestation. However, if there is any severe nutrient deficiency in the soil, or if it is too acidic, then this should be amended before planting.

1. Loosen the soil with a garden fork, or a deep-ripper for larger areas.

2. Throw the seeds down, making sure there are enough to eventually keep weeds out.

3. Rake them in, covering them with soil up to three times the width of the seed – push down gently. It also helps to cover them with a light layer of mulch.

4. Make sure they have enough water to get started, and irrigate if the soil becomes dry.

5. When the first ones start to flower cut them all and cover with a light layer of mulch so their nitrogen is not lost to the air. (If you cut them a lot later they will use up a lot of nitrogen from the soil in the production of flowers and seed, but will have produced a lot more carbon to use as mulch.)

What to Grow

It helps to have a mixture of nitrogen-fixing plants, such as cowpea, and a grain crop, such as Japanese millet. The legume provides the nitrogen and the grain provides lots of organic matter and carbon. Choose crops that suit your area.

Before planting, many legumes need to be inoculated ('mixed') with the *Rhizobium* bacteria selected for that plant and a bit of water. This helps them generate nitrogen more effectively. When buying seeds ask if you need to get the inoculant as well (about $7 per packet, or free if you buy the seeds from Green Harvest). They usually come with instructions. Inoculants look like black soil and need to be stored in the fridge to stay alive. Don't confuse it for the miso or you'll be having a different form of living soup for dinner.

Nitrogen-fixing Green Manure Crops

Warm season:	Cool season:
Cow pea	Broad beans
Lablab	Chick peas
Lentil	Fenugreek
Mung bean	Lupins
Soy bean	Peas – field, dun or tic
	Subclover
	Woolly pod vetch

Grain Green Manure Crops

Check which ones suit your area.

Warm season:	Cool season:
Buckwheat	Barley
Japanese millet	Canola
Sorghum	Oats
	Ryecorn
	Wheat/Triticale

Grow a Cover Crop

Unlike a green manure crop, a cover crop is a perennial carpet that regrows after being cut back. Often it doesn't even need to be cut and can still be attractive. They keep out weeds, protect fruit trees from aggressive grass, stop the need to spray, prevent erosion, attract beneficial predators and reduce the need to mow. The living carpet keeps the soil temperature more even and because the soil is not compacted by mowing it attracts a large range of soil life.

To keep predator habitat and give weeds less chance, grow a combination of winter vigorous and summer vigorous crops. Research the best crops for your area.

Permaculture mainly focuses on perennial plants as these require a lot less work and the results last much longer.

Pinto peanuts are a great orchard groundcover as they fix nitrogen, attract bees, tolerate partial shade and most importantly don't need mowing.

Living Mulches

(Many of these species and the green manure seeds are available from Green Harvest, along with helpful free information sheets.)

Barrel medic	Red clover
Crown vetch	Shaw creeping vigna
Lotononis	Villomix
Lucerne/afalfa	White clover
Maku lotus	Wynn's cassia
Pinto's peanut	

Build the Swale of the Century

Swales can change a dry garden into a lush oasis that doesn't rely on your sweat to moisten it.

If sloping areas shed water quickly, they dry out. Swales are large, shallow ditches that run along the contour of the land (or slightly off contour) and catch water running downhill, holding it for a couple of hours, even days. This gives the water time to filter into the soil and spread over a wide area. Swales can be small or large and are made at intervals depending mainly on the steepness of the slope and soil-type. Water run-off from tank

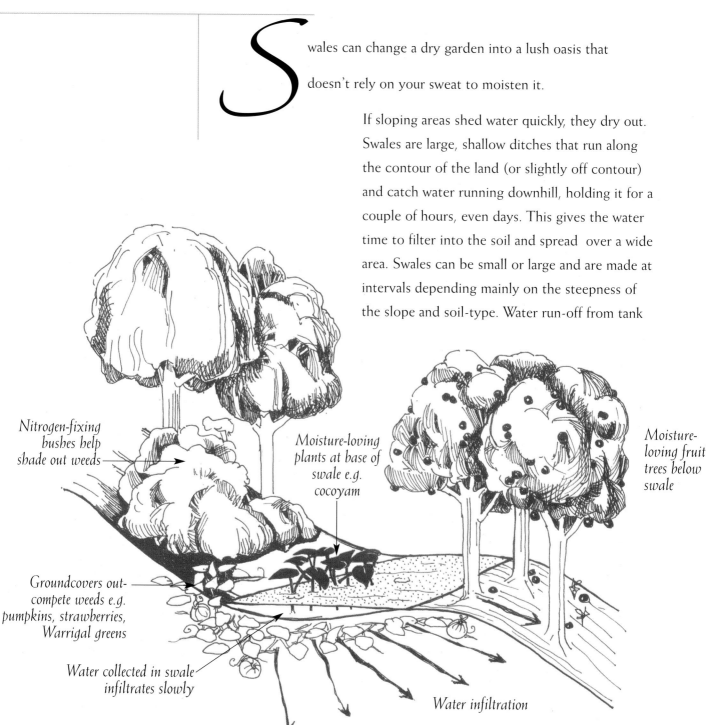

Nitrogen-fixing bushes help shade out weeds

Moisture-loving plants at base of swale e.g. cocoyam

Moisture-loving fruit trees below swale

Groundcovers out-compete weeds e.g. pumpkins, strawberries, Warrigal greens

Water collected in swale infiltrates slowly

Water infiltration

overflows, roof areas, roads and other hard surfaces can be directed into swales.

If the soil is heavy and doesn't absorb water well, incorporate gypsum in (and above) the swale. Alternatively, aerate the soil with a garden fork or a deep-ripper. A deep-ripper is a machine that breaks up the soil but doesn't turn it over.

If making an earth swale, reduce potential erosion by planting a green manure or cover crop into the newly exposed soil. This can also add nitrogen to the soil and keep out weeds. If there is a chance of heavy rain, mix the crop with a fast-growing grain that will hold the soil together quickly, such as Japanese millet. This remarkable crop can start sending roots down in four days.

Below the swale, plant moisture-loving trees. Plants that can handle dry conditions, such as olives, can be planted above the swale or on the swale lip if it is above the infiltration level. Be aware that the lip can dry out and shallow-rooted plants can suffer, especially if they're young and haven't yet sent their roots into the moist areas.

To avoid difficulties in managing grass or weeds in the swales, plant them up fully and mulch well. At all stages of development aim to have lots of groundcovers, bushes and trees, with few gaps in between.

If you can't make a swale but want to improve filtration, then create a contour of:

- ridges of soil
- lines of tightly packed rocks
- rows of close deep-rooted plants, such as comfrey
- ridges of mulch.

Swales can also be used on either a small or large scale to direct water away from areas of high-water concentration (gullies) and towards more dry areas (ridges). To do this run swales slightly downhill from the more moist areas across to the dry areas. By spreading the water, larger areas of moist growing conditions are created and fewer plants are exposed to the extremes of flooding or drought.

On steep areas swales also create more flat, arable land and provide niches for plants that may not be able to grow there otherwise.

When making the swale, either by machine or hand, first place the topsoil to one side, dig the rest and then put most of the topsoil back onto the flat area and some onto the sloping banks. This way the topsoil is not mixed up with the subsoil and much of its value lost.

Strawberries, Warrigal greens, golden marjoram, thyme

Slopes 5° back

Slightly off contour to drain off storm water

Living in Your Paradise

For the moment, put the vision of your garden aside. Visions

can sometimes blind you to what is already there. Let's take a

different approach. Let us leap into the present garden

moment….into a state of complete acceptance…away from

relentless striving. There are no weeds to pull, no wilting plants

to water, no jobs hanging half finished. It's just the way it is.

The handsome tailed-emperor butterfly.

The present is a real, in-the-moment child's space. Genuine wonders, wonders invisible to the future-focused eye: a spider carefully packing up its dewy threads after a night of fishing; the exploratory red velvet horns of the citrus butterfly caterpillar; a skink gleaming like polished brass on a sunlit path — more delicate that any artisan can sculpt.

Sell your cleverness and buy bewilderment.

Jalal ud-Din Rumi

Take time to appreciate the beauty of a 'pest' in its natural habitat and the melody and glint of the wrens they attract.

Lay back, gaze unthinkingly at the sky and partially glimpse a city of insects where a thousand tiny beating wings rise like mist.

Only when there are no nagging thoughts, no 'musts and shoulds', only when you stop, will you see that your life depends on the tens of chewing beetles and caterpillars; the hundreds of sucking aphids; thousands of worms; millions of springtails; billions of unseen phagocytes, budding yeasts and darting flagellates; and trillions of cilia that beat ceaselessly through watery films over what once was living. The cycle of death is life's vital other half.

Living in paradise involves understanding that the fresh smell of moist soil is a broth of decay, reconstituting life and transforming it into the fragrant juice of delicious fruits. You, your thoughts and dreams are also the fruits of that soil.

Savour the taste of an orange; reflect on the mysteries of your garden. Forego a glass of juice from each tree so that beautiful and exquisite 'pests' can flourish, as vivid as the lamellose wings of the citrus butterflies. Many insects are

Transport pathways of a leaf, like an urban street map.

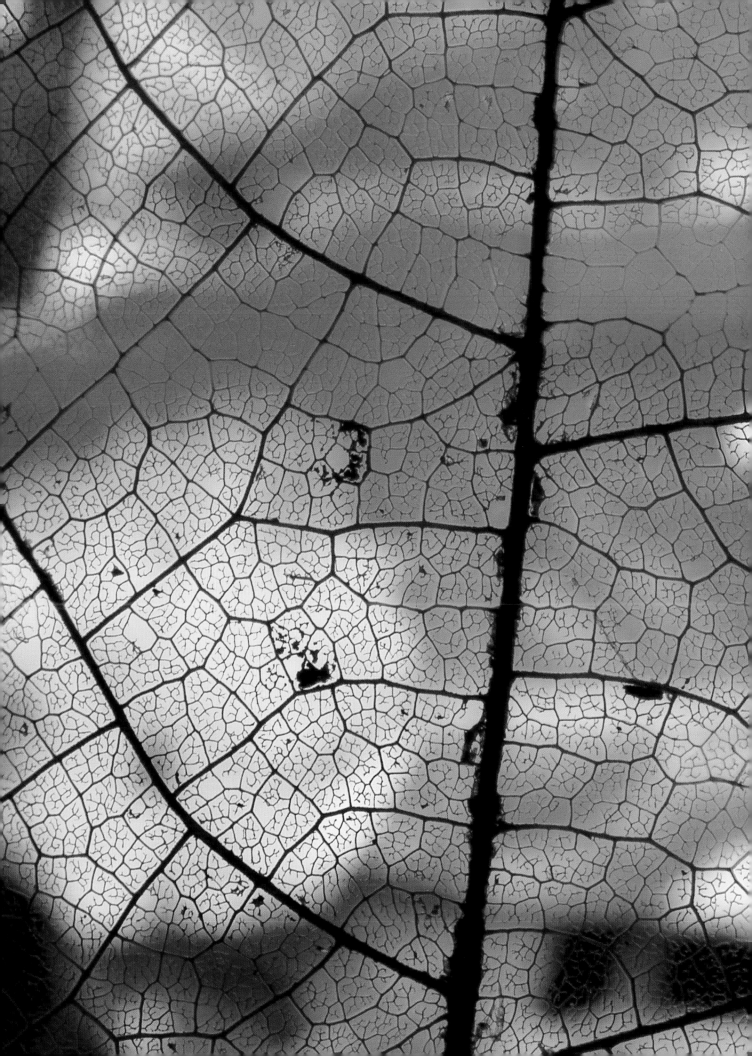

The illuminated gills of ephemeral fungi.

actually your friends, preying on pests — enjoy the iridescent spectacle of a summer chalcidoidea wasp as it dances with wind-touched elegance. Its existence near the top of the insect food chain is testimony to your garden's health.

Recognise that you're no more important in the garden ecosystem than a mud wasp or fairy wren. You can help influence and shape your paradise, but you can never own it.

Sit with humility. Nature is often forced to yield to human misjudgements, but she will bounce back to amend oversights with resources at hand: weed seeds, chewing mandibles, piercing ovipositors, parasites and diseases.

As the sun sets, luminescent fungi start to glow.

Eavesdrop on a frog singing lesson.

Paradise is not a standard of living to achieve, but a quality of life to enjoy. The paradisiacal can be a stimulating and integral feature of your daily sensory intake. Watch, feel, taste, smell, listen.

Listen is an anagram of silent. In silence the wind whispers to you. Feel it caressing your neck and face. Developing a garden in partnership with nature leads to a rich and untamed relationship.

If at times you're in doubt what to do next in the garden, sometimes it's best to just wait. Respect nature and she will to come up with the answer. While you wait, take the opportunity to quietly celebrate the wonders of your garden… as it is now.

Epilogue

As you can appreciate, designs are a dynamic process and as I grow, my design grows with me. By documenting the garden over time I see how it reflects my life's whims. When I bought the property seven years ago I was in pragmatic mode. I wanted food pronto — herbs, vegetables, bush foods, fruit and to quickly plant my cabinet timbers so I wouldn't wait any longer than 25 years for my dowry. One year later I had time to rest.

We think we are creating paradise, but maybe paradise is creating us.

I created the meditation seat, the swinging chair overlooking the dam, the seat for viewing the vegie garden and the fire-circle. I put up the hammock. Then the next year my partner arrived (did the hammock play a role?) Correspondingly the sexual organs of plants — flowers — emerged. Initially lipstick reds and bright yellows; later, to becalm the mood, we interspersed cooler whites and liquid blues. The natural follow-up was domesticity — the cooking adventure — as we conjured up gourmet delights from India, the Middle East and Vietnam. Up popped the curry tree, the cinnamon tree, the kaffir lime, Lebanese cress, Vietnamese mint, sweet leaf bush, lots of coriander, and the 'oys': pak-choi, bok-choi, choy-sum and tatsoi. Oy, what's next? Vegetarian seafood perhaps, and we'll be proud of our great shocks of seaweed, anchored by coral, their tendrils streaming like destiny down salt-water falls! Just joking.

Useful Resources

Information

Queensland

Global Ecovillage Network (Oceania), Crystal Waters, MS 16 Maleny, Qld 4552 Tel: (07) 5494 4741, Fax: (07) 5494 4578, www.gaia.org/thegen/genoceania/index.html Has information and workshops on Ecovillages in Australia and the rest of the world.

Rare Fruit Council of Australia, PO Box 715, Aitkenvale, Qld 4814 Join and receive their great magazine with details on rare species and how to grow and eat them.

Sustainable Futures, 50 Crystal Waters, MS 16 Maleny, Qld 4552 Tel: (07) 5494 4833 e-mail: info@permaculture.au.com, www.permaculture.au.com Weekend and two-week permaculture workshops, and a selection of interesting ecological books.

New South Wales

Exotic Fruitgrowers Association Ltd, PO Box 399, Alstonville, NSW 2477

Landcare Groups — Australia. Tel: (02) 9412 1040, Fax: (02) 9412 1066 Join your local Landcare group to find out about trees native to your area, weed management, tours etc.

NSW Nutgrowers Association, PO Box 281, Goulburn, NSW 2580

Organic Herb Growers of Australia, PO Box 6171, South Lismore, NSW 2480 Tel: (02) 6622 0100, www.organicherbs.org

Permaculture Research Institute POB Shannon Tel: (02) 6688 6222 PRI@permaculture.org.au www.permaculture.org.au Networking, courses, research.

Victoria

Heritage Fruits Group, Permaculture Melbourne, 6 Derby Street, Kew, Vic. 3101 Tel: (03) 94994232

Victorian Nutgrower's Association, GPO Box 2196T, Melbourne, Vic. 3001

WWOOF (Willing Workers On Organic Farms), Mt Murrindal Co-Op, Buchan, Vic. 3885 WWOOFERS (unfortunate name) work for four hours per day in return for board and keep.

Tasmania

Tagari Publications, publishers for the Permaculture Institute since 1979. The primary function of Tagari Publications is to help support the work of the Permaculture Institute by publishing and selling books about sustainability and then transferring profits to the Permaculture Institute.

Tagari Publications may be contacted at the Permaculture Institute, 31 Rulla Road, Sisters Creek, Tas. 7325, Australia. Tel: (03) 6445 0945; Fax: (03) 6445 0944; tagariadmin@southcom.com.au

In addition to a wide range of permaculture and related books, the Permaculture Institute offers courses with Bill Mollison.

South Australia

Adelaide Rare Fruit Society, 45 Northampton Cres., Elizabeth East, SA 5112 Tel: (08) 8252 3929

South Australian Nut and Tree Crops Association,184 Longwood Road, Heathfield, SA 5153

Western Australia

Western Australian Nut and Tree Crop Association, PO Box 27, Subiaco, WA 6008 Tel: (08) 93881965 www.aoi.com.au/wanatea

New Zealand

Permaculture in New Zealand permaculture@eartheal.org.nz

New Zealand Tree Crops Association, PO Box 1542, Hamilton

United States of America

California Rare Fruit Growers, Fullerton Arboretum, CSUF, Fullerton, California, 92634

Living Off The Land, PO Box 2123, Melbourne, Florida, 32902-2131

North American Fruit Explorers, Route 1, Box 94, Chapin, Illinois, 62628. Exotic temperate fruit.

Rare Fruit Council International, 3280 South Miama Avenue, Miama, Florida, 33129

Interesting Plants

Including uncommon fruits, nuts, bush foods, native plants, vegetables, bamboos and aquatic species.

Queensland

Earthcare Enterprises, Bamboo and aquatics, Hans Erken, PO Box 500, Maleny, Qld 4552 www.earthcare.com.au

Fairhill Native Plant Nursery, Fairhill Road, Yandina, Qld 4561 Tel: (07) 5446 7088 Largest range of native plants in Queensland www.fairhillnursery.com

Green Harvest Organic Mail Order Supplies, 52 Crystal Waters, Maleny, Qld 4552 Tel: (07) 5494 4676 www.greenharvest.com.au Freecall 1800 681014 Specialists in Natural Pest

Management. Suppliers of seeds and plants, tools, accessories and books. Useful information sheets available. Order their free catalogue, *Australian Organic Gardening Resource Guide.*

Isabel Shippard's Herb Farm, Nursery and Mail Order, PO Box 66, Nambour, Qld 4560 Large range of herbs. Can deliver throughout Australia.

New South Wales

Bundanoon Village Nursery, 71 Penrose Road, Bundanoon, NSW 2578 Tel: (02) 4883 6303 Lots of fragrant plants, rare bulbs, herbs and unusual food plants.

Sunraysia, 45 Stuart Highway, Gol Gol, NSW 2738 Tel: (03) 5024 8643, www.sunraysianurseries.com.au A broad selection of grape varieties, and many unusual citrus, olives and other fruit trees.

The Fragrant Garden, Portsmouth Road, Erina, NSW 2250 Tel: (02) 4367 7322 Many types of herbs including fragrant, medicinal, culinary and dye. Direct sale and mail order.

Victoria

Badger's Keep, Chewton, Vic. Tel/Fax: (03) 5472 3338 Historic apple varieties.

Dragonfly Aquatics, RMB AB 366, Colac, Vic. 3249 Tel: (03) 5236 6320. A wide range of aquatic and water edge plants, both edible and ornamental.

Kuranga Native Nursery, 393 Maroondah Highway, Ringwood, Vic. 3134 Tel: (03) 9879 4076 www.kuranga.com.au Wide range of bush food trees. Bush food information kit also available.

Tristania Park Nurseries, 28 Homour Avenue, Macedon, Vic. 3440. Tel: (03) 5426 1667. Bare-rooted deciduous fruit trees available June–August.

Vamina rare plants, 25 Moores Road, Monbulk, Vic. 3793 Tel: (03) 9756 6335 An excellent variety of rare plants.

Tasmania

Bob Magnus, Woodbridge, Tas., 7162 Tel: (03) 6267 4430 Apples and 15 varieties of grafted quinces.

South Australia

Australian Bush Products, PO Box 131, Strathalbyn, SA 5255 Bush food seeds and seedlings by mail order.

Perry's Fruit and Nut Nursery, Kangarilla Road, McLaren Flat, SA 5571 Tel: (08) 8383 0268 www.perrysfruitnursery.com.au

Vadoulis Garden Centre, 554 Main North Road, Gawler, SA 5118 Tel: (08) 8522 3400 Bush food trees available.

New Zealand

Koanga Gardens, RD2, Maungaturoto, New Zealand. Tel: (0011 64) 94312145

Treedimension Nursery, Box 211, Motueka, New Zealand. Tel: (0011 64) 3528 8718 Common and unusual fruits and nuts.

King's Herb Haven, 1660 Great North Road, Avondale, Auckland, New Zealand

Seeds

Queensland

Eden Seeds, MS 316, Gympie, Qld 4570 Tel: (07) 5486 5230 Eden Seeds distribute traditional, open-pollinated vegetable seeds.

New South Wales

Greenpatch Organic Seeds, PO Box 1285, Taree, NSW 2430 Tel: (02) 6551 4240

Rainforest Seed Collective, PMB, Bellingen, NSW 2454

Seed Saver's Network, PO Box 975 Byron Bay, NSW 2481 Tel: (02) 6685 6624 www.seedsavers.net Rare and special plants, biannual newsletter and plant swapping, biodiversity news. Collects, catalogues and maintains open-pollinated non-hybrid seeds, specialising in traditional vegetable varieties.

Victoria

Broersen Bulbs, 365–7 Monbulk Road, Silvan, Vic. 3795 Tel: (03) 9737 9202 www.broersen.com.au

Digger's Club Seeds, 'Heronswood', 105 Latrobe Parade, Dromana, Vic. 3936 Tel: (03) 5987 1877 www.diggers.com.au Excellent mail order seed catalogue, wide range of heirloom and specialist seeds such as capsicums specifically for cooking, tomatoes for drying. Join the club.

Heritage Seed Curators Association, PO Box 1450, Bairnsdale, Vic. 3875 Wide range of hard-to-find fruit and veg including tree tomato, persimmon, kiwi fruit and olive.

New Gippsland Seeds and Bulbs, PO Box 1, Silvan, Vic. 3795. Tel: (03) 9737 9560 www.possumpages.com.au/newgipps/index.htm

Tasmania

Phoenix Seeds, PO Box 207, Snug, Tas., 7054 Tel: (03) 6267 9663 A broad and exciting range of self-replicating seeds.

Western Australia

Bay Seed Garden, PO Box 1164, Busselton, WA, 6280 Tel: (08) 9752 2513

Recommended Reading

Allen, Jenny and Knudsen, Barb, 1996, *Eat Your Garden Video: Create a Permaculture Oasis*, Jenny Allen, Maleny

Baxter, Paul, 1997, *Fruit Growing In Australia For Profit or Pleasure*, Pan Macmillan, Sydney

Deans, Esther, 1977, *Esther Deans' Gardening Book: Growing Without Digging*, Harper and Row, Sydney

Fanton, Michel and Jude, 1994, *The Seed Saver's Handbook*, Seed Savers' Network, Byron Bay

Furuno, Takao, *The Power of Duck: Integrated Rice and Duck Farming*, Tagari Publications, Tasmania

Glowinski, Louis, 1999, *The Complete Book of Fruit Growing in Australia: Over 200 Temperate and Subtropical Fruits, Nuts and Berries to Grow in Gardens, Farms or Orchards*, Lothian Books, Melbourne

Hangay, George and German, Pavel, 2000, *Insects of Australia*, Reed New Holland, Sydney

Kourik, Robert, 1986, *Designing and Maintaining Your Edible Landscape Naturally*, Metamorphic Press, USA

Low, Tim, 1999, *Feral Future — The Untold Story Of Australia's Exotic Invaders*, Viking, Melbourne

McMaugh, Judy, 2002, *What Garden Pest or Disease Is That? Organic and Chemical Solutions For Every Garden Problem*, Reed New Holland, Sydney

Mollison, Bill, 1990, *Permaculture: A Practical Guide For a Sustainable Future*, Tagari Publications, Tasmania

Mollison, Bill, 1997, *Introduction To Permaculture*, Tagari Publications, Tasmania

Mollison, Bill, *Permaculture: A Designers' Manual*, Tagari Publications, Tasmania

Mollison, Bill, with Reny Mia Slay, *Introduction to Permaculture*, Tagari Publications, Tasmania

Mollison, Bill, *Permaculture Two: Practical Design for Town and Country in Permanent Agriculture*, Tagari Publications, Tasmania

Mollison, Bill, *The Permaculture Book of Ferment and Human Nutrition*, Tagari Publications, Tasmania

Mollison, Bill, *Travels in Dreams: An Autobiography*, Tagari Publications, Tasmania

Olkowski, W. et al, 1991, *Commonsense Pest Control — Least-toxic solutions for your Home, Garden, Pets and Community*, Taunton Press Inc., USA

Osler, Mirabel, 1989, *A Gentle Plea for Chaos*, Bloomsbury Publishing, London

Simons, Margaret, 1999, *Wheelbarrows, Chooks and Children: A Gardener's Life*, New Holland, Sydney

Timms, Peter, 1999, *The Nature of Gardens*, Allen and Unwin, Sydney

Windhust, Allan, 1994, *Worms Downunder For Farm, Garden, Schools, Profit and Recycling*, Allscape, Mandurang, Victoria

Woodrow, Linda, 1996, *The Permaculture Home Garden: How to Grow Great-tasting Fruit and Vegetables the Organic Way — and Enjoy Every Minute Of It*, Viking, Ringwood

Woodward, Penny, 2000, *Asian Herbs and Vegetables: How to Identify, Grow and Use Them In Australia*, Hyland House Publishing, Flemington

Photo Credits

Botanical Names and Potential Weeds

* = potential weeds

Permaculture often aims to grow plants that are low-maintenance, hardy and competitive. However one person's successful plant may well be another's nightmare weed. In this book I have tried to avoid mentioning many species that fall into this category, yet some I have because they are safe to grow in many regions or if managed properly. Any of these plants that may have weed potential are asterisked here. If you plan to grow any of them, first make sure they don't have weed potential in your area and that you are also willing to manage them so they don't become weeds. You will find a large number of species are asterisked — this is because I'm thinking of worst case scenarios and don't like the idea of any more weeds in this country. In Tim Low's book *Feral Future*, he explains how weeds in Australia account for more devastation than all our mines combined. Sadly, this great book reads like a Stephen King horror.

Acerola cherry – *Malpighia glabra*

Ageratum – *Ageratum houstonianum* *

Apricot – *Prunus armeniaca*

Aloe Vera – *Aloe barbadensis*

Anise – *Pimpinella anisum*

Aniseed Myrtle *Backhousia anisata*

Arrowroot – *Canna edulis* *

Asparagus – *Asparagus officinalis* *

Atherton almond – *Athertonia diversifolia*

Avocado – *Persea americana*

Babaco *Carica pentagona*

Bamboo – *Bambusa* spp. *

Bangalow palm – *Archontophoenix cunninghamiana*

Barrel medic – *Medicago truncatula*

Black bean – *Castanospermum australe*

Blue eye – *Evolvulus pilosus*

Caraway – *Carum carvi*

Carob – *Ceratonia siliqua*

Carol myrtle – *Backhousia myrtifolia*

Cat's whiskers – *Orthosiphon aristatus*

Catmint – *Nepetea cataria* *

Chamomile – *Chamaemelum nobile* *

Chilli – *Capsicum* spp. *

Chinese Star jasmine – *Trachelospermum jasminoides* *

Chocolate pudding fruit – *Diospyros digyna*

Choko – *Sechium edule* *

Clover – *Trifolium* spp. *

Coastal banksia – *Banksia integrifolia*

Cocoyam – *Xanthosoma sagittifolium*

Coffee – *Coffea* spp. *

Coltsfoot – *Tussilago farfara* *

Comfrey – *Symphytum officinale* *

Corduroy tamarind – *Arytera lautereriana*

Coriander – *Coriandrum sativum*

Cowpea – *Vigna unguiculata*

Crotalaria – *Crotalaria grahamiana* *

Crow's ash – *Flindersia australis*

Crown vetch – *Coronilla varia*

Curry leaf tree – *Murraya koenigii* *

Custard apple – *Annona cherimola*

Date palm – *Phoenix dactylifera*

Davidson's plum – *Davidsonia pruriens* var. *jerseyana*

Daylily – *Hemerocallis fulva*

Dill – *Anethum graveolens*

Dinosaur gourd – *Lagenaria* spp.

Dragon fruit (pitaya) – *Hylocereus guatemalensis* *

Elephant ears – *Xanthosoma*

sagittifolium *

Feijoa – *Feijoa sellowiana*

Fennel – *Foenicilum vulgare* *

Fig – *Ficus carica* *

Finger lime – *Microcitrus australasica*

Fish plant – *Houttuynia cordata*

French tarragon – *Artemisia dracunculus*

Galangal – *Alpinia galanga*

Garlic – *Allium sativum*

Geranium – *Pelargonium* spp. *

Giant laulau – *Syzygium megacarpa*

Ginger – *Zingiber officinale*

Granadilla – *Passiflora ligularis* *

Grumichama – *Eugenia brasiliensis*

Guava – *Psidium guajava* *

Guisaro – *Psidium guineense*

Ice cream bean – *Inga edulis* *

Jaboticaba – *Myrciaria cauliflora*

Jackfruit – *Artocarpus heterophyllus*

Japanese millet – *Echinochloa utilis*

Japanese pumpkin – *Cucurbita moschata* and *Cucurbita maxima*

Japanese raisin tree – *Hovenia dulcis*

Jerusalem artichoke – *Helianthus tuberosus* *

Juncus – *Juncus* spp. *

Kaffir lime – *Citrus hystrix*

Kangaroo grass – *Themeda australis*

Kangaroo paw – *Anigozanthos* spp.

Kangkong – *Ipomea aquatica**

Kiwi fruit – *Actinidia chinensis*

Lablab – *Lablab purpureus**

Lebanese cress – *Aethionema curdifolum**

Lemon balm – *Melissa officinalis*

Lemongrass – *Cymbopogon citrates*

Lemon verbena – *Lippia citriodora*

Lemonade fruit – *Citrus limon* x *Citrus limon* var. *Meyer*

Lemon-scented myrtle – *Backhousia citriodora*

Lentils – *Lens culinaris*

Licorice – *Glycyrrhiza glabra*

Lilly pilly – *Acmena smithii**

Longan – *Euphoria longan*

Loquat – *Eriobotrya japonica**

Lotononis – *Lotononis bainesii*

Lotus – *Nelumbo nucifera**

Lucerne/alfalfa – *Medicago sativa*

Lupin – *Lupinus alba*

Macadamia nut – *Macadamia integrifolia/tetraphylla**

Macaranga – *Macaranga tanarius*

Maidenhair fern – *Adiantum aethiopicum*

Maku lotus – *Lotus uliginous*

Mango – *Mangifera indica**

Marjoram – *Origanum* spp.

Midyim berry – *Austromyrtus dulcis*

Mint – *Mentha* spp.*

Miracle fruit – *Synsepalum dulcificum*

Mizuna – *Brassica rapa* var. *nipposinica*

Monsteria – *Monstera deliciosa*

Mt Morgan silver wattle – *Acacia podalyrifolia**

Mulberries – *Morus* spp.*

Mushroom plant – *Rungia klossii*

Nasturtium – *Tropaeolum majus**

Native coral tree – *Erythrina vespertilio*

Native crotalaria – *Crotalaria* spp.

Native jasmine – *Pandorea jasminoides**

Native lasiandra/blue tongue – *Melastoma affine*

Native mulberry – *Piptureus argenteus*

Native pepper – *Tasmannia insipida*

Native pultenea – *Pultenea* spp.

Native tamarind – *Diploglottis australis*

Native violet – *Viola hederacea**

Night-scented jessamine – *Cestrum nocturnum**

Oats – *Avena sativa**

Okra – *Abelmoschus enculentus*

Olive – *Olea europea**

Oregano – *Origanum* spp.

Panama berry – *Muntingia calabura*

Passionfruit – *Passiflora edulis**

Pawpaw – *Carica papaya*

Peanut butter tree – *Bunchosia argentinia*

Pecan – *Carya illinoenis*

Penny royal – *Mentha pulegium**

Pepino – *Solanum muricatum*

Peppermint – *Mentha piperita**

Peppermint geranium – *Pelargonium tomentosum*

Persimmon – *Diospyros kaki*

Philodendron – *Philodendron bipinnatifidum*

Pigeon pea – *Cajanus cajan**

Pineapple guava – *Feijoa sellowiana*

Pineapple sage – *Salvia elegans**

Pine nut – *Pinus* spp.

Pinto peanuts – *Arachis pintoi*

Pistachio – *Pistacia vera*

Pomegranate – *Punica granatum*

Poppy – *Papaver* spp.

Protea – *Protea* 'Pink Ice'

Pomelo – *Citrus maxima*

Queen Anne's lace – *Ammi majus**

Quince – *Cydonia oblonga*

Raspberries/rose-leaf marara – *Rubus rosifolius**

Red cherry guava – *Psidium cattleianum**

Red clover – *Trifolium pratense**

Rocket – *Eruca sativa*

Rose apple – *Syzygium jambos*

Rose geranium – *Pelargonium graveolens*

Russian garlic – *Allium ampeloprasn*

Sage, purple – *Salvia officinalis* 'Purpurea'*

Sandpaper fig – *Ficus coronata*

Shaw creeping vigna – *Vigna parkeri*

Siberian pea tree – *Caragana arborescens*

Small-leaved lilly pilly – *Syzygium leuhmannii*

Snake beans – *Vigna unguiculata* ssp. *sesquipedalis*

Snake gourd – *Trichosanthes angina*

Society garlic – *Fulbaghia violacea*

Star apple – *Chrysophyllum cainito*

Sweet granadilla – *Passiflora ligularis*

Sweet leaf bush – *Sauropus androgynus**

Sweet lillicoy – *Passiflora alata*

Sweet potato – *Ipomoea batatus**

Tagasaste – *Chamaecytisus proliferus**

Tamarillo or tree tomato – *Cyphomandra betacea*

Tatsoi/choy sum – *Brassica rapa* var. *rosularis*

Thyme – *Thymus* spp.

Tiger lily – *Lily tigrinum**

Tumeric – *Curcuma longa*

Vietnamese mint – *Persicaria odorata**

Villomix – *Aeschynomene villosa*

Walnut – *Juglans* spp.

Warrigal greens – *Tetragonia tetragonoides**

Water chestnut – *Eleocharis dulcis**

Watercress – *Nasturtium officinale**

Waterlily – *Nymphaea* spp.*

Water spinach – *Ipomoea aquatica**

White clover – *Trifolium repens**

White sapote – *Casimiroa edulis*

White sweet Alice/alyssum – *Lobularia maritime**

Woolly pod vetch – *Vicia villosa*

Wynn's cassia – *Cassia rotundifolia*

Yarrow – *Achillea millefolium**

Yellow cherry guava – *Psidium littorale* var. *littorale**

Yucon/sweet fruit root – *Polymnia sonchifolia*

Zigzag wattle – *Acacia macradenia*

Index